THE LOVING PARENTS' GUIDE TO DISCIPLINE

THE LOVING PARENTS' GUIDE TO DISCIPLINE

How to Teach Your Child to
Behave Responsibly—With Kindness,
Understanding, and Respect

MARILYN E. GOOTMAN, ED.D.

BERKLEY BOOKS, NEW YORK

This book is an original publication of The Berkley Publishing Group.

THE LOVING PARENTS' GUIDE TO DISCIPLINE

A Berkley Book / published by arrangement with
the author

PRINTING HISTORY
Berkley mass market edition / February 1995
Berkley revised and updated trade paperback edition / August 2000

The Penguin Putnam Inc. World Wide Web site address is
http://www.penguinputnam.com

ISBN: 0-425-17450-6

BERKLEY®
Berkley Books are published by The Berkley Publishing Group, a division
of Penguin Putnam Inc., 375 Hudson Street, New York, New York 10014.
BERKLEY and the "B" design are trademarks belonging to Penguin Putnam Inc.

PRINTED IN THE UNITED STATES OF AMERICA

10 9 8 7 6 5 4 3 2 1

Acknowledgments

Many very special people have helped make this manuscript a reality:

My dear friend Gail Karwoski launched me into the writing profession. She convinced me I could be a writer and then guided and encouraged me through the process.

Carol Kurtz is another dear friend. Her enthusiasm, genuine love, and professional and personal insights have enriched my manuscript and my life.

Freyda Siegel is not only my aunt but my mentor as well. Freyda has a magical touch with children and parents. Every step of the way, I have consulted with her in writing this book. Most of the scenarios in this book are Freyda Siegel originals.

I have been fortunate to share the parenting experience with my husband, Elliot. In addition to being my partner and soul mate, Elliot is also my first reader and editor. His clarity and organization have helped me tremendously.

My three children, Elissa, Jennifer, and Michael, have given me on-the-job-training for writing this book. Elissa also provided me with skillful editorial assistance. I have been blessed to witness my children blossoming into responsible, caring adults.

CONTENTS

CHAPTER ONE

What Is Discipline?

The child stared at the shiny red apples stacked neatly before him. He looked up at the glaring peddler. His large brown eyes skirted back and forth between the pushcart's juicy red apples and its menacing owner.

"Hey, kid, are you trying to steal my apples?" shouted the peddler.

"Oh, no, sir," said the little boy, trembling. "I'm trying hard not to!"

Discipline is indeed hard for children. But discipline is also every bit as hard for parents. In fact, for many, discipline is *the* most difficult aspect of parenting.

YOU CAN LEARN HOW TO DISCIPLINE SUCCESSFULLY

We live in a fast-paced, instant society: instant food, instant printing, instant weight loss. We have become spoiled and expect to get what we want when we want it. Certainly it would be nice to achieve instant discipline, for discipline can consume much time

1

and energy. But instant discipline works about as well as instant weight loss programs. They work for a while, but soon we end up at our starting point, sometimes even worse off, gaining back more weight than was lost. The diet programs that succeed where others fail do so because they are based on the premise that new habits must be slowly formed and reinforced. Behavior must change gradually if it is to remain changed. Anyone who claims to have an all-purpose, instant solution to discipline is selling snake oil. People just don't work that way.

But neither does discipline have to be viewed as a fearsome, burdensome chore. Any parent can learn how to discipline without memorizing lists of behaviors and strategies. As you practice the discipline skills taught in this book, you will soon find that you will be able to apply them naturally in your own way. This practical, realistic approach to discipline is easy to apply in most situations. From my own experience and that of countless other parents, I know that with practice, this approach to discipline takes some of the stress out of parenting and helps both parents and children feel good about themselves. This is truly discipline that works!

WHAT IS DISCIPLINE?

The underlying premise of this book is that discipline is helping children develop self-control. All children start life not knowing any of the skills of self-control, yet they need to learn them in order to become independent, responsible, happy, well-adjusted members of a democratic society. Remember, children come into this world totally naked and helpless—physically, socially, and emotionally. As parents, we have to teach our children the self-control they will need to successfully make it in the world on their own. Children have to learn how to take care of their own needs, how to protect their own health and safety, how to cope with disappointment, how to share, how to express themselves constructively, how to feel good about themselves, and how to respect the needs of others and get along with them.

Fortunately both for us and our children, learning self-control is a slow, gradual process. We don't have to teach our children how to survive and thrive in this world overnight. We have about eighteen years to transfer the responsibility from us to them. The amount and kind of self-control we teach our children changes as they grow. When we discipline our children, we must consider what they are capable of doing and understanding at a particular age and stage of development. Ten-year-olds can clear their plates and wash their own dishes, but one-year-olds can't. Sixteen-year-olds can go out alone in the evening with their friends, but ten-year-olds shouldn't. As children grow older, they should be capable of assuming more responsibilities and privileges. Ironically, the opposite is often the case. Many children are given more responsibility and independence at seven than at seventeen. Many seven-year-olds are allowed to bike around the neighborhood, visiting and playing with whomever is available as long as they return by a certain hour. By the time they are seventeen, however, they are often expected to give a detailed account of exactly when and where they are going.

DISCIPLINE DOES NOT MEAN PUNISHMENT

Often when parents are asked how they discipline their children, they respond with how they punish them; but discipline is guiding, encouraging, building self-esteem as well as correcting misbehavior—everything we do to help our children become the best that they can be. Punishment focuses only on misbehavior. The goal of discipline is to teach children how to do the right thing. The goal of punishment is to teach children not to do the wrong thing. Good discipline certainly requires that children experience the consequences of their misbehavior, and that includes punishment at times, but punishment is only one thread in the fabric of discipline. We discipline our children by setting limits, giving them responsibility, boosting their self-esteem, and teaching them how to solve problems and make good judgments. These are the discipline skills taught in this book.

Sometimes parents punish children by making them do something unnecessary and distasteful just "to build character." Resentment rather than character building is usually the outcome. Children have ample opportunities to build their character in the process of daily living—friends reject them, they have hours of homework, they don't get chosen for a team. . . . Discipline should be meaningful and purposeful. It should emerge from the context of daily life. It need not be imposed and artificially created.

WHY SPANKING SEEMS EASIER BUT REALLY ISN'T

Spanking is a very emotional topic. Many parents who were spanked believe that they should spank their own children. Many feel they have to defend their own parents for spanking them. Our parents did the best they could, but times have changed. We know more than they did about the negative side effects of spanking. We know more about how to discipline successfully without spanking. If we can set aside our emotions and look at the facts, we will see that we can be more successful today in bringing up our children if we find alternatives to spanking.

Sometimes children's behavior is so frustrating and annoying that it may be tempting to spank them. It may seem easy at the time, but the long-term price is high. Babies who are hit often cry louder and louder. The problem only gets worse. Older children who are hit often learn to solve problems by hitting others. Many become bullies and pick fights, concluding that big people can hit little people.

Many parents become enraged and spank on the spur of the moment, not because they had planned to but because they are uncontrollably angry and they don't know what else to do. This teaches their children to lash out on the spot without thinking. There are indeed alternatives to spanking that are far less distasteful and that work much better. A child who breaks a window playing ball too close to the house will learn a lot more from having to pay for the window than from being spanked.

Some parents spank to be sure that their children know who's boss. Children do need to know that the adult is in charge. But while spanking can teach children to be afraid of the adult in charge, good discipline teaches them to respect him or her.

Spanking can make children afraid to misbehave, but probably only when their parents are watching. Children need to learn to control their own behavior even when parents are not around to see what they are doing. Discipline helps children learn how to control their own behavior.

Some parents feel that children simply need a good spanking sometimes. No child needs a spanking. Spanking can be dangerous. You can never tell when a child will be hurt badly by a spanking if we lose control. Children do not need to be hit in order to learn how to behave.

Spanking does not teach children how to change what they do, as good discipline should. Many parents notice that, after a spanking, children may settle down for a while, but pretty soon they start misbehaving again. Some children use spankings as an easy way to take away their guilt. They figure they can do what they want, get spanked, have a clean slate, and do whatever they want all over again. Effective discipline holds children accountable for their actions and puts the responsibility onto them for changing their own behavior, as with the child who had to pay for the broken window.

WITH DISCIPLINE, PARENTS ARE TEACHERS

When our children come into this world, they are physically helpless. Newborn babies cannot survive without assistance. They don't know how to feed themselves, clothe themselves, keep themselves clean or safe. It's no wonder so many new parents feel overwhelmed by having to assume all these responsibilities for their children. Fortunately, infancy does not last forever, and we can gradually teach our children how to take care of themselves by slowly shifting the responsibility from us to them. We can teach one-year-olds to hold their own cups, two-year-olds to feed themselves, twelve-year-olds to fry an egg, and sixteen-year-olds to cook dinner. Two-year-olds can learn to take off their shoes, six-year-olds to tie them, and fifteen-year-olds to buy them. We can teach preschoolers to avoid the street, ten-year-olds how to cross the street, and sixteen-year-olds how to drive on the street.

Just as our children enter this world physically helpless, they enter it socially and emotionally helpless. They don't know that they can't have everything they want when they want it, how to get along with others, or how to solve their own problems. They don't even know how to feel about themselves. Just as we can teach our children to take care of their own physical needs, we can teach them how to emotionally and socially cope on their own. Little by little we can slowly transfer the responsibility from us to them. Two-year-olds can learn to play near other toddlers. Five-year-olds can learn to play not just near but with their friends. Eight-year-olds can learn to play games with rules, and eighteen-year-olds can vote.

Parents can learn skills that will help them teach their children to be self-disciplined. Each of these skills is thoroughly explained in this book. Real-life examples and practice activities are plentiful.

TIMES HAVE CHANGED

Many people are skeptical about the need to learn skills. After all, our parents managed to bring us up without reading books and taking courses. Why can't we just do the same? We can't because times have changed. We live in a new era, an era of changing family structure, media bombardment, violence, drugs, and the struggle for individual rights.

Thirty or forty years ago, many households resembled the television show *Leave It to Beaver*. Father was the head of the household. Mother stayed home, doting on both father and children. Children seemed to live less stressful lives. Today, many fathers share household responsibilities, most mothers work outside the home, and many children now live with only one parent. For the most part, we no longer have extended families to relieve us in times of stress. Far more pressure is placed on today's parents and children, both with respect to time and responsibility. Busy parents need their children to behave responsibly both when they are around and when they are not. Time is very precious in today's busy world. Many parents do not have time for extensive parenting courses yet would like to improve their parenting skills. The skills in this book can be learned in a minimal amount of time.

In addition to our changing households, children are changing as well. Today's children, even the very young, are no longer naive and innocent. They see anything and everything on television, far more than is healthy for them to handle. Children are not emotionally equipped for all that comes through "the tube." Many become overstimulated, jumpy, irritable, and fearful. As a result, they misbehave.

Today we have an urgent, life-threatening need to teach our children survival skills. Our parents were spared from having to deal with the horrors of violence, drugs, and problems such as AIDS. Our children, though, face many temptations and obstacles that did not exist in our day. We have to teach them the skills of self-control, of taking responsibility for oneself. Learning self-discipline can be a matter of life and death for them. They must learn the self-control to behave not only in our presence or when we might find out what they did, but at all times. The approach in this book teaches us how to help our children withstand today's pressures through self-discipline. It teaches us how to help our children solve their own problems. Simply telling our children to "just say no" does not work.

In the past, discipline was based on authority. Children did not question, they did not demand to be heard. Today, children know that they have rights and are unafraid to speak up for them. Disciplining them becomes more challenging. We have to justify our actions and be more responsive to our children's concerns. Giving people a voice in a democratic society does not make life easier, just better. But parents have rights also, and they must retain the right to be the ultimate authority. This book is sensitive both to the rights of children and to the rights of parents. Both parties must be treated with respect and dignity.

A final challenge to parents' decisions about discipline is that many of us do not agree with our own parents' approaches to discipline. We were angry and resentful as children. We promised that we would never discipline our children the way they disciplined us, whether it was sending us to bed without dinner, embarrassing us in public, or hurting us physically. "When I grow up, I won't do that to my kids," we vowed. However, our parents' approach, undesirable though it may have been, was all we knew. Slowly we found ourselves treating our children the same way. Changing out of a comfortable old shoe, ragged and worn though it may be, is difficult. However, at some point, for our own well-being and that of our children, we have to try to reconsider our approach. Such is the case with ineffective discipline methods that we learned from our parents. We can draw on our past experience, examine our current approaches, learn new skills, and revise our behavior accordingly.

ALL CHILDREN NEED TO BE TAUGHT DISCIPLINE

Discipline is a fact of life, a normal part of the process of growing and developing. "Why can't my kids just behave so that I won't have to discipline them?" is a common parental cry. Every single child comes into this world not knowing the ropes. All children need to be taught discipline. No child exists that is well-disciplined without being taught. How else will they know what is expected? Often, children who seem to be misbehaving are merely ignorant of the proper way to act in a given situation. We cannot take it for granted that children will know how to behave if we have not guided them. During his 1992 visit to Australia, President Bush smiled and flashed the "V for victory" sign throughout the streets only to discover later that that gesture has a totally different, insulting meaning in that country. Of course, he did not mean to be offensive. No one had taught him how to behave in Australia.

Teaching children what is expected at their age, teaching them how to behave, teaching them the rules of the land, is only half of what parents have to do when disciplining their children. Discipline also involves correcting misbehavior. While growing up, all children will make mistakes, some more so, others less so; but all children will mess up at one time or another and misbehave. There are many reasons why children misbehave—immaturity, ignorance, and rebelliousness, among others. These will be discussed later in more detail. Whatever the cause, we need to discipline children; we need to establish consequences for their misbehavior and teach them how not to repeat the same mistake. Here is where the skill of problem solving plays a major role.

This book focuses on two aspects of discipline: how to teach our children the skills of appropriate behavior and how to teach our children to avoid inappropriate behavior. Both are essential facets of successful discipline. This approach takes some of the distastefulness out of discipline. When discipline is viewed only as punishing misbehavior, it can be quite unpleasant and discouraging. Misbehavior should not be viewed as a failure in the discipline process. Every instance of misbehavior should be viewed as an opportunity to continue and further the teaching of self-discipline.

Discipline is not something we do *to* our children, but rather discipline is something we do *with* our children as part of the process of teaching them self-discipline.

SUCCESSFUL DISCIPLINE TAKES PRACTICE

We can learn how to discipline just like we can learn any other skill—by study and practice. If we wanted to learn how to use a computer, we would probably read a book that explains it, study the examples and illustrations, and practice exercises in the book. Finally, we would start using the computer. Periodically, we might return to the book for further guidance, to refresh our memories, or to focus on an aspect we missed the first time around. We can take the same approach with discipline—inform ourselves about the meaning and techniques of discipline, do practice exercises alone or with another adult pretending to be a child, and then try it out in real life with our children, returning at times to refresh or improve our skills.

You may feel awkward at first trying out this new approach. The more experience you get, the more it will become second nature to you. After attending a workshop on communicating, I tried using some new approaches with my children. After a few tries, one of my children said, "Okay, what technique are you trying out on us now?" She was right; I was trying out something new on them. But it didn't matter. I explained that I was trying to learn how to become a better parent and kept it up. After a while, the new way of communicating became second nature to us.

Practice is like putting money in the discipline bank for those times when we need to make an urgent withdrawal. If we are bankrupt, with no skills stored up, we might act impulsively, lash out, and regret it later. Sometimes when we don't know how to react to a child who misbehaves, we say and do irrational things that only get us deeper and deeper into conflict. Better still, knowing that we had skills stored in our bank, we could have stepped back from the situation a moment and taken time to think about which skill we would withdraw to solve the problem.

THERE ARE NO SUCH MONSTERS AS PERFECT PARENTS OR PERFECT CHILDREN

Many parents worry about their every word and action, fearing that they will scar their children for life if they do or say the wrong thing. We are human. Imperfection is part of the human condition. We must be genuine and sincere, but not perfect. It's okay if we mess up at first. We need not worry about every mistake we make. Children are flexible. We have plenty of opportunities to correct our mistakes and many years to teach them discipline. The key is to realize when we have gone astray, try to pick up the pieces, think through the problem and possible solutions, apologize if necessary, and try again, keeping in mind that our ultimate goal is helping our children develop self-control. It is to be expected, too, that children will make mistakes and not always respond. We must just persist with them and help them learn to become their own problem solvers.

Many of us have become paranoid about every word that comes out of our mouths. I have seen parents speaking to their children as if they were reading from a script, devoid of emotion and feelings but saying the correct words. They seem to be afraid that someone is lurking around the bend, monitoring every word and action. Nobody has the right to tell you what to say and think. You should not have to treat a parenting book like a bible, referring to specific pages every time you run into a problem.

GOOD DISCIPLINARIANS ARE NOT PALS TO THEIR CHILDREN

Certainly, we all want to have a warm, loving relationship with our children, but we need to set boundaries. Parents and children are not equal in age, experience, or authority. If we are pals to our children, we may not be able to get respect when we need it.

DISCIPLINE SEEMS HARD

Growing up is a slow, gradual process. Fortunately, we don't have to teach our children how to survive and thrive in this world all at once. As we've said before, we have about eighteen years to transfer the responsibility from us to them. Even if several of those years have passed, it's never too late to start teaching children discipline. Teaching discipline is not just a one-time event. It may be harder at first for someone who starts when children are older, but it can be done. If you are trying a new approach on older children, let them know what you are doing. Let them know you are sincerely trying to be a better parent, more sensitive to their needs. Remember, to effectively discipline our children, we must do it *with* them, not *to* them.

Perfect parents and perfect children do not exist. We can and will make mistakes. Our children can and will make mistakes. Mistakes are part of the learning process for both us and our children.

Many parents feel teens need more discipline than their younger children. With effective discipline skills, the opposite is the case. As our children grow and develop, they should become increasingly less dependent upon us for guidance and more dependent on their inner selves.

Raising children is a difficult job, but as children learn to control their own behavior, discipline gets easier and easier. It's well worth the initial effort as our children become responsible for their actions. And we can feel proud that our loving care guided them on their way.

Teaching children discipline is like planting a tree. The labor is intense at first. Little seedlings need constant care. They need to be propped up to grow straight and tall. They need water and protection from the elements. As their roots dig deep in the earth and their trunks extend high into the air, they can thrive on their own, finally providing shelter and shade to others.

SUMMARY OF MAIN POINTS

* Parents can learn skills for discipline so that their children will develop and grow into productive, happy adults who competently face life on their own.

* Discipline is a fact of life, a normal part of the process of growing and developing.

* Discipline is something we do *with* our children, not do *to* them.

* Discipline is helping our children develop self-control in a way that allows them to feel good about themselves.

* Discipline is far more than punishment.

* Spanking may seem easier but does not work in the long run.

* Misbehavior provides an opportunity for learning self-discipline.

* Successful discipline takes practice.

* Successful discipline takes time.

* Problem solving for both parents and children is an important aspect of successful discipline.

CHAPTER TWO

Setting the Stage

"All the world is a stage
And all the men and women merely players"

—William Shakespeare

The world is indeed a stage. And when it comes to the lives of our children, we parents can help set the stage so that our children will find it easier to take on the role of a well-behaved person. As stage directors, we can help organize their space and time and model for them what we consider to be appropriate ways of acting.

ORGANIZATION

By organizing space and time for our children, we can take a major step in avoiding some discipline hassles.

Space: There's a Place for Everything

Getting children to clean up after themselves can be a discipline nightmare.

Mike and Andy are having a glorious time playing. First they build towers and castles with their Legos. Next they go on to do a few puzzles. Then out come the blocks and toy cars. Soon they are drawing with colored markers. Suddenly a voice calls in the distance, "Boys, it's time to clean up." Five minutes later, Mom appears at the door, looks at the mess, and exclaims in total exasperation, "I mean clean up right now . . . right now or else!" But how can they possibly clean up that mass of dislocated toys and puzzle pieces? To Mike and Andy, it may seem as if Mom has asked them to climb Mount Everest.

Shelves, containers, and labels to the rescue! These organizational tools can save us parents countless hours of threatening, pleading, and punishing, "Clean up your room or else. . . ." Separate containers for toys that come in many pieces and set spots for each toy make it easier for children to put things in their proper place.

Children can get in the habit of putting things where they belong if their possessions have set spots that are convenient. Coatracks and hooks for book bags placed near the door make it convenient for children to use them when they come in the house. Hampers in their rooms rather than in the bathroom make it less likely that dirty laundry will end up on the floor of their room. Bringing dirty clothes to the bathroom can be an inconvenience, but reaching over to the hamper in their room can be manageable (not for all kids—I have one child who would not feel comfortable if her room were too neat—but for most).

However, just having organizational props is not enough to prevent the discipline cleanup nightmare. As stage directors, we also have to teach our children how to use these props. Kids can't be expected to know how to put everything away by themselves— they need our help. "Let's find all the puzzle pieces and place them in this box. Now let's put the Legos in the Lego box. Now let's . . ." Teaching them how to tackle and put away one item at a time helps them learn how to do this on their own in the future. This way we can teach them how to take responsibility for their possessions and save ourselves many discipline hassles.

Space: Hide the Temptations

Imagine sitting down at a table in front of a huge piece of scrumptious-looking chocolate cake only to be told not to touch it. It certainly would be a challenge not to at least nibble a little crumb here and there. The whole world is like one big piece of chocolate cake to children, and they want to taste every bit of it. They want to run, touch, and explore with abandon. What they explore differs by the age, but at all ages kids explore and experiment. Look what happens here:

DAD: *There you go again, Ben! Touching something you've been told not to touch. Now you've broken an expensive vase.*

BEN: *I'm sorry, Dad. I didn't mean to break it. I just wanted to see it. It was an accident, really it was.*

DAD: *But, Ben, I told you to stop playing with it. Why didn't you just leave it in the box?*

BEN: *Because I wanted to see it.*

DAD: *You just never listen! You are so disobedient.*

BEN: *But I just wanted to—*

DAD: *You never do as you're told.*

A younger child may be curious about a new vase while an older child may be just as curious about the wine in the refrigerator. For our children's own safety and for the safety of our possessions, we need to take direct action to steer this marvelous inquisitiveness in the direction of appropriate behavior. Fences keep children from running into the street, cabinets keep breakables out of their reach, electric covers keep them from getting shocked. Why leave temptations staring them in the face?

Some parents of young children find it helpful to clear off the bottom shelves in their bookcases and place children's books on these shelves. When children have their own special space, they are less likely to trespass onto the adult space. Setting aside one drawer or cabinet in the kitchen for toys and kitchen equipment that are appropriate for child's play can keep a young child occupied constructively while Mom or Dad cooks. Plastic drinking cups spare parents anxiety about breakage and encourage independent eating habits.

Older children also benefit when temptations are not staring them in the face. If there's no junk food in the house, they'll have to find something else to eat. They are more likely to use restraint in drinking if alcohol usage is kept to a minimum at home. You might ask, shouldn't children learn self-control and not to touch something when we tell them not to? Yes, they should. But there are so many temptations we cannot put out of their reach, we don't need to maintain available temptations just for the sake of teaching them to obey us. By removing the temptations we have control over, we can concentrate our efforts where they are truly needed.

Time: There's a Time for Everything

Setting routines involves establishing both a time schedule and procedures. Routines help children know what is expected of them and when. Routines eliminate us as parents from having to say the same thing over and over again and having to explain everything anew every day. They are valuable cues for helping children learn how to behave appropriately. When we set routines, children know what we expect of them and get the opportunity to practice the appropriate behavior daily. Good habits then become automatic. Having established routines for bedtimes, meals, and chores eliminates many discipline problems.

Setting up a time schedule for daily activities is the first step for establishing routines. "I don't want to go to bed yet. I'm not tired. It's too early" and "I'm busy playing. I don't want to eat" are all too familiar comments. However, if times are established for bed and meals, responding to these comments becomes easier: "Remember, we eat at six o'clock"; "Remember, bedtime is eight o'clock." There's less room for negotiation and argument this way. If there aren't set times, many children will frequently choose to argue and nag about bedtime or coming to the table. Also, without time schedules, children may begin to think that they can do anything they want whenever they want to, not a helpful attitude for living in society.

After setting up a consistent time schedule, it is helpful to establish procedures, what to do when the time arrives:

Eating: washing before eating, setting the table, cleaning up afterward

Sleeping: cleaning up toys, brushing teeth, settling-down activities such as reading

Doing homework: gathering books and supplies, establishing a consistent location

Watching television: how much time allowed, which shows allowed, what must be done first

Sleep-overs: how many, which nights acceptable

Routines help children feel safe. They know what is expected of them. When kids live in chaotic homes where there are no routines and everything is decided on the spur of the moment, they never know what is expected of them, so they are on guard all the time. And when they're on guard, they become extremely jumpy and sensitive—hardly an ideal situation for good discipline.

Routines are helpful, but rigidity is not. "No, you cannot watch the inauguration of the President, it's past your bedtime," and "No, you can't go to the fair with your friends. We eat supper at that time," are unreasonable responses. Routines do not have to be etched in stone. We do not want our children to become rigid, inflexible people. We must be flexible in our routines, revising them for exceptional situations, explaining when and why we are changing them. Also, we should be willing to explain why we generally do not change them.

Here are some suggestions for using routines to help avoid discipline problems:

• Determine whether your children understand the pattern of your routines. If not, explain the routines to them. (Sometimes it may seem obvious to us but not to our children.)

• When the routines change—either temporarily, perhaps for a special occasion (such as when guests are visiting and bedtime is made later that evening), or permanently (such as when they get older and their bedtime gets later)—clearly explain the changes to your children.

Time: Smooth the Transitions

Many children have a hard time going from one activity to another. Warning them a few minutes ahead of time helps them get ready and avoids discipline problems that arise when they are not ready. Just as stage managers may announce, "Five minutes to curtain time," so, too, we should announce, "You have five more minutes before bedtime." "We'll be eating supper in ten minutes." Then, if Brian's busy making the Eiffel Tower just before supper, he has enough time to figure out a good stopping point in his construction.

Time: Allow Enough of It

Time has a different connotation for children than it does for us adults. Children live in the present; they do not have our experience with deadlines or our notion of time as limited. We hurry them, yet they persist in taking their time. When possible, it's helpful to allow a little more time than we think they'll need, such as for getting dressed. When young children, in particular, are rushed, they tend to feel rejected. Besides, rushing them isn't necessarily going to get them to move any faster.

Checklists: A Tool for Time Organization

Checklists are an organizational tool that can teach our children self-discipline and take some of the burden off of us parents. With our help, our children can make a list of things they need to do when they come home from school. Then they can check each item off as it is completed. For example:

_____ hang up coat and book bag
_____ have snack
_____ clear dishes from snack
_____ relax
_____ do homework
    _____ math
    _____ reading
    _____ social studies
    _____ science
    _____ spelling
    _____ writing
_____ do chores
    _____ take out trash
    _____ make bed

A dry erase board where children can list these activities, check them off each day as they are accomplished, and then the next morning erase the checks and start over is a system many children and parents have found helpful. Others find it helpful to print a list of activities on card stock paper and laminate it. That way, children can check off items each day, wipe it off at the end of the day, and then start anew the next day. The use of lists not only helps us avoid nagging and behavior problems, it also helps our children learn good school habits. Keeping lists of assignments and setting aside specific time for completing them are important habits for succeeding in school.

We may have to walk our children through the steps of checking off items on the list as each item is accomplished. We may have to help them both create and revise their checklists. In addition, many children need to be reminded to refer to their lists. But with our guidance along the way, children can learn to use checklists and save us much nagging and punishing.

Summary

Helping our children organize their space and time makes life more pleasant for all of us. When children know where things belong, they are more likely to put them there. When temptations are not staring them in the face, children are less likely to reach for them. When children know what to do, they are more likely to do it.

MODELING

Modeling is another way we direct our children to correct behavior. We are the models for our children, who copy our behavior. This phenomenon is much to our advantage, as it saves us from having to teach our children every little detail of how to act in life—a seemingly endless task. Modeling is a terrific tool for teaching kids discipline, but it's also a tricky tool. There are two sides to the coin. Children copy our undesirable behaviors as well as mimic our noble ones.

Often we don't even realize when we are sending off two conflicting messages to our children, when we are telling them to act one way, but are modeling another way of behavior. A father admonishes his child for using a cussword: "How many times have I told you not to use that kind of language?" The child responds, "But, Daddy, it's the same word you used last night when the car cut in front of you. . . ." Actions speak louder than words. When a conflict arises between what we say and what we do, our children will usually choose to copy what we do rather than what we say.

We can use our behavior as an example for our children and save ourselves from many discipline headaches. Five areas where this is particularly helpful are maintaining cleanliness, admitting mistakes, relating respectfully, being honest, and keeping our cool.

Cleanliness Is Next to Godliness

Mrs. Robbins comes home from work, places her coat on the back of the chair, and remarks that she'll be leaving in an hour to go to a meeting. She then plops down into her favorite chair to read the newspaper. She tears out a few important stories she would like to save, puts them on the lamp table next to her, leaves the rest of the papers in a pile on the floor, and then goes off to the kitchen to prepare supper. Right after the family finishes eating, Mr. Robbins excuses himself, saying he's very busy, and retires to his desk to do some work.

Mom tells her children to hang up their clothes and then finds an excuse to leave hers slung across the back of a chair. If she tells her children to put their toys away but then leaves her newspapers lying around the house, what do you think they will do—follow her directions or her actions? If Dad stresses the importance of everyone pitching in to clean up, yet he uses the excuse of work to avoid cleaning up, then why shouldn't the children use the excuse of homework to accomplish the same end?

Let's think of our children's point of view. How can they understand this double standard?

MOM: *Todd, come help me straighten up the living room.*
TODD: *Do I have to, Mom?*
MOM: *Yes, you do! I'm expecting company, and I'm in a hurry to get through. I need your help.*
TODD: *But I didn't mess it up.*
MOM: *That makes no difference, Todd. As a member of the family, you have to pitch in and help when help is needed.*
TODD: *But you don't help me, Mom!*
MOM: *What do you mean, I don't help you?*
TODD: *You don't—you never do.*
MOM: *Don't I cook for you, buy you things, drive you to activities? What do you mean, I don't help you?*
TODD: *But when I ask you to help me pick up my toys, you always say, "Do it yourself, they're your toys!"*
MOM: *That's different!*
TODD: *Why is it different?*
MOM: *Because it is. That's why!*

Mom expects Todd to perform on command, to cooperate and help out when she tells him to. Yet, when Todd asks for help, she tells him to do it by himself, probably thinking that this way she can help him develop his independence. The truth is, it is no different for a child to ask for help with a task than it is for the parent to ask for help with a task. Both should have the right to assistance when necessary. We may not have time to help them. That's okay. But they should have a right to ask and receive the help when it is convenient for us to give it to them. In this way, we can teach our children a valuable lesson in cooperation.

Take a few minutes to think about your own habits and ask yourself:

- Are my standards for cleanliness different for me than for my children?

- Do I put my possessions away immediately after I use them?

- Do I moan and groan about all the work I have to do?

- Do I pitch in and help out other members of the family when I can?

To Err Is Human

Mrs. Gray turns her children's rooms upside down looking for her good scissors. She is sure one of her children borrowed them and neglected to return them. "I can never find anything around here. You're always taking my things and then not putting them back where they belong. I need those scissors to cut this fabric. Don't ever take anything of mine again." Despite their protests, she insists that they must have misplaced the scissors. A few days later, she finds the scissors on a shelf where she hastily placed them the previous week when someone came to the door. How does she confess this to her children? "I found my scissors on the shelf—but I had good reason to suspect you since you usually do take them" or "I'm sorry I accused you unfairly. I left the scissors on the shelf." Mrs. Gray's response will determine how her children respond to their own mistakes. Will they be willing to admit that they messed up and go on from there, or will they deny their mistakes or blame them on someone else?

Many parents find it difficult to apologize to their children even when an apology is in order. Yet children are frequently commanded to "say you're sorry" even when they do not feel the slightest bit of remorse. Every single human being on this earth makes mistakes. If we can admit when we make mistakes, then our children will feel comfortable doing so, also.

The most common discipline concern I have heard voiced by both parents and teachers alike is: What do I do after a child misbehaves? The first step is getting children to admit that they have messed up, that they have done something wrong. They will be much more likely to do so if we, too, are willing to admit when we mess up and do something wrong. Our children will follow our lead.

The Respect Boomerang

Respect is like a boomerang. If we send it out, we will get it back. If we speak politely to our children, they will speak politely to us (usually!). We all have our lapses, including and especially children. We can't expect that our children will be respectful at all times even if they do respect us in general. That's too much to ask. If we are honest with our children, they will be honest with us (usually!). If we speak with kindness and sensitivity, they will speak with kindness and sensitivity (usually!). If we take them seriously (and not laugh at them), they will take us seriously. As we sow, so shall we reap.

Realistically, we cannot expect that our children will always treat us with respect. Many factors may get in the way—they want to look "cool" in front of their friends, they're frustrated and angry, and they lose control. We must confront these situations directly when they occur and nip them in the bud. However, if we treat our children respectfully, these situations will be few and far between and can be dealt with constructively.

Some parents think that to gain their children's respect, they have to be very strict and impose harsh punishments if their children disobey them. "I let my kids know just where they stand. They'd better respect me, or they'll be in big trouble." These parents confuse respect with fear. Children who are afraid of their parents often become resentful and sneaky. Many seek ways to avoid their parents' decrees or sneak around them.

When children are treated with respect, they are much more

likely to respect their parents and cooperate with them. Respect means treating our children as we would want to be treated. We don't like to be yelled at, humiliated, threatened, or spoken to sarcastically, so why should children? Children are quite fragile and depend on us to help them build up self-confidence and courage to face the world. Respect and self-respect go hand in hand.

It might be helpful to ask the following questions to help gauge the extent to which we are sending out the respect boomerang:

- Do I use the same manners with my children as I do with adults?

- Am I honest with my children?

- Do I speak to them in kind tones?

- Do I avoid sarcasm, humiliation, and terror tactics?

- Do I take my children seriously and refrain from laughing at their ideas and thoughts?

Honesty and Sincerity Are the Best Policy

Mother walks up to the ticket booth with thirteen-year-old Jennifer. "Two tickets, one adult and one under twelve."

Dad uses his business charge card for the hotel on the family vacation.

Mom copies a computer program from her office and uses it for her own personal use.

Mom and Dad decide not to tell their children that their grandfather is sick.

Parents may justify these kinds of lies in their minds, but if it's okay for Mom and Dad not to tell the truth sometimes, then why shouldn't their children? It is difficult for children to define a "white lie," and they often understand it to be any kind of lie they may use to protect themselves or to gain a benefit. This can become a discipline problem. Our children may misbehave, break a rule, and then decide to cover it up with a "white lie." They figure, if it's okay for parents, then why not for them? One major problem is that their moral and value systems are not yet fully developed. This behavior can get them into a lot of trouble. Our own honesty is the best safeguard for avoiding discipline problems that arise out of dishonesty.

Keeping Our Cool

Parenting can certainly be stressful. Our children can push us to our limits. Sometimes we may feel so angry that we feel like a volcano about to explode. But if we do explode and let our rage splatter on our children, we not only make them fearful of us but we also teach them that this is the way to handle anger. Trying our best to keep our cool and learning to express our anger constructively (see chapter 6), teaches our children to do the same. Children do as we do.

Summary

"Am I behaving the way I am expecting my children to behave?" is the key question to ask ourselves as we look in the mirror. Remember, actions speak louder than words. Try to become aware of some of your children's most annoying habits that create discipline problems for you. Then take a look in the mirror. Are they merely reflecting back what they see?

SUMMARY OF MAIN POINTS

• We parents can provide the props and cues that signal to our children how they should behave and prevent some discipline problems in the process.

• By organizing space and time for our children, we can take a major step in avoiding some discipline pitfalls.

• We can use our own behavior as an example for our children and save ourselves many discipline headaches, especially when it comes to maintaining cleanliness, admitting mistakes, being respectful, and fighting fairly.

• Our own honesty is the best safeguard for avoiding discipline problems that arise out of dishonesty.

CHAPTER THREE

Rules and Limits

The following analogy provides us with a framework for our discussion of rules and limits:

The hikers trudged through the woods to reach a magnificent waterfall. The path up was steep and their hunger and exhaustion growing, yet they forged ahead, propelled by the exciting prospect of seeing the waterfall. Their anticipation was building as they neared their destination. Up one hill, then another, over a few rocks and slippery spots, and then they were there. They finally arrived only to find a huge barricade blocking most of their view. On it was posted, Danger. Do Not Pass Beyond This Fence. Fuming, they ranted and raved about the park wardens—how could they be so insensitive? Didn't they realize how important the view was to hikers? One hiker vowed to get back at them and wrote obscene messages all over the barricade. Another, blinded by his fury, decided to scale the eight-foot fence—he was going to see the waterfall regardless. He may have seen the waterfall, but does not recall anything about the moments before his twenty-foot plunge.

A second group of hikers trudged through the woods to another waterfall. Up one hill, then another, over a few rocks and slippery spots, and then they were there—ah, what a view! Straight before them, in all its raw beauty, was a raging waterfall. A fine mist of refreshingly cool water sprayed their faces. But one hiker became panicky. "What if I slip? What if I get too close and fall down the slope?" He cowered near the path, unable to relax until they descended. One of his friends, however, was fascinated by the waterfall. He edged closer and closer to get the best possible view, until . . .

A third group of hikers trudged through the woods to yet another waterfall. They all ran up to the waist-high fence, held the rail, and gazed with awe at this majestic scene. A gentle cool mist sprayed their faces as they relaxed, soaking up the beauty that lay before them.

So, too, as they hike through childhood, do our children need waist-high fences to keep them safely on the path to adulthood. They need waist-high limits, limits that will provide them with safety and security as well as the freedom to enjoy life. Many parents assume that when disciplining their children they have before them two options—to be permissive and build no fence for the protection of their children or to be strict and build huge barricades. Just as with the hikers, neither of these approaches works.

UNREASONABLE BARRICADES: HOW KIDS RESPOND

"I have to have strict rules. I don't want my child getting into any trouble." "Strict rules breed character." "My children need to know who's boss." "If I don't have strict rules, my children will walk all over me." These are some parents' justifications for excessively strict rules. They are captains who run an overly tight ship, often being strict just for the sake of being strict, thinking that this will teach their charges discipline and self-control. However, when children have unfairly strict rules, they often rebel—it is mutiny on the home front.

Here are some ways children respond to unreasonable barricades:

"You Can't Make Me"

As we saw with the hikers, huge barricades that close us off from independence and enjoyment can breed fury, not obedience. When parents are unfairly and overly strict, many children seethe inside. Some get back at their parents by symbolically writing on the barricades—through back talk, destructiveness, poor schoolwork, defiance, and hurtfulness. One sixth grader, enraged at having to go to bed at eight o'clock each night, periodically let the air out of one of his mother's tires. Other children hurdle the barricades, misbehaving more than they would if the rules were reasonable. One teen who had a ridiculously early curfew came home on time, went "to bed," then climbed out his window into the waiting arms of his girlfriend.

"Whatever You Say"

Strict parents proclaim: "My children should obey me instantly because I'm the parent and I know what's best." "This is my house, and I'm in charge. What I say has to go." "They need to know who's boss." "If they don't obey me, then they won't obey their teacher." These parents demand blind obedience. But children who are taught to obey adults without thinking are at risk. Why? Because these children may blindly obey any authority figure, even one who may do them harm. "Whatever you say" is their response to all adults. Certainly, most parents would not endanger their own children; but, unfortunately, other adults may. Children must think before they act and not allow themselves to be intimidated by an authority figure who commands them to do something harmful that is not in their best interest. Obedience is certainly desirable, but blind obedience can have serious negative ramifications.

"You'll Never Know"

"I have to be strict because I can't trust my child." Excessively strict rules often breed sneakiness. Children who do not understand the reasons for rules and suspect that they exist because their parents don't trust them will figure out clever ways of getting around these barricades. One sixteen-year-old whose parents would not let her date would arrange to meet her boyfriend at the movies each weekend. Paradoxically, when parents are overly strict because they do not trust their children, their children often respond with sneakiness and untrustworthiness, hoping "you'll never know." While some rules may make sense, when they are enforced rigidly, children often respond with sneakiness. A third grader who was not allowed to ever chew gum removed the already chewed gum from the bottoms of desks in school and chewed it. Another child who was never allowed to eat candy used his allowance to buy candy on the way to school and then ate it at school.

NO FENCES: HOW KIDS RESPOND

Setting limits for children can be challenging for parents. Some don't want to make their children unhappy, but having no rules can be just as harmful to children as having excessively harsh rules. Here are some ways children respond when there are no fences:

"I Need It Now!"

"They're only kids; childhood should be a time of much joy and few demands." "If I don't give her what she wants, she'll think I don't love her." "I don't want him to throw a fit." "I have to get him one; everyone else has one." These are the justifications given by permissive parents who place few if any restrictions on their children. However, reality is such that we cannot have everything we want and when we want it in life. Every single human being on this earth must cope with restrictions, frustration, and disappointment as part of normal living. Therefore, we need to gradually help our children learn how to cope. If we give in to children and do not enforce rules that are important just because we don't want to get them upset, then we are not preparing them for life's reality. Well-adjusted members of society are those who have learned to accept limitations and adversity so that they can live in harmony with others and be sensitive to the needs and feelings of those around them. Impatient, demanding adults who insist "I need it now" often have a hard time coping with life; they are often unhappy and make others unhappy as well.

"I'm Afraid"

"I don't want my children to feel restricted." "I don't have time to explain rules." "It's not worth the hassle." These are other excuses given by parents who set down no rules or limits for their children. If permissive parents do not set down limits, their children will never know the security that structure can provide. Imagine the feeling of being at the edge of the waterfall, not knowing just how far you could safely venture forward before meeting with disaster! Without the fence limits provide, some children lack any self-confidence. They cower in the corner of life, afraid to take risks, afraid to experience their childhood to the fullest.

"Stop Me"

Other children keep searching for the fence. They push and push, getting closer and closer to the edge to find the security of the boundary, not unlike the way cattle do when placed in a pasture. They act out, perhaps even becoming destructive to themselves or others. They are crying for limits, for guidance, for structure—begging for someone to "stop me." Unfortunately, for many, the limit cannot be found until they have already fallen over the edge. We should not wait until the principal, police officer, or psychiatrist has to set down the limits for our children.

"You Don't Care"

"I don't have to set limits because I'm sure my children have enough sense to do the right thing," claim some parents. But children are novices at life. Most children, including teens, consider themselves to be immortal. They are oblivious to the real dangers that exist in this world. Regardless of how responsible and trustworthy they are, all children still do need the protection of limits.

Ironic though it may seem, many children interpret their parents' lack of limits as a lack of caring. Children do not see the world as we do. They filter their experiences through their own youthful, immature concepts. My teenaged daughter was complaining to her friend about her curfew for a particular evening when her friend shot back, "At least your parents care enough to want to know when you'll be home! My parents don't ask me where I'm going and don't even know when I'm home."

WAIST-HIGH FENCES: HOW KIDS RESPOND

When we establish and explain reasonable rules that respect their dignity and feelings, our children are more likely to respect us. Here are some common responses to reasonable rules and limits:

"I Get It"

We stop at stop signs because we know that they are there to protect ours and others' safety. However, if stop signs were placed all along a one-way street with no intersections, we would be tempted to pass by them without stopping. If our rules are meaningful so that they are not irrationally restrictive, our children will be much more likely to obey them.

Even if a police officer is not around, we stop at stop signs because we understand their importance for our safety and the safety of others. Even if we are not around, our children will be more likely to obey our rules if they understand their importance.

"I Feel Safe"

Imagine being at the edge of that waterfall and not having a protective fence! Children are novices in this world; they don't know how close to the edge they can get without getting hurt. Even though they often won't admit it, children need to know that someone cares enough to set down limits that will keep them safe and secure.

"I Can Handle It"

Living in society means living with rules that are set up for the benefit of all. Sometimes that means that we cannot have what we want when we want it or that we cannot do something we would like to do. Right from the start, we must teach our children how to cope with limitations that are necessary for living with others, even though it may restrict them. They need to know that "I can handle it, even if I'm frustrated and disappointed."

HOW TO BUILD THE WAIST-HIGH FENCE

Setting reasonable limits does require thought, understanding, and experimentation. Rules should vary with the age and stage of the child. It is appropriate to expect a five-year-old to hold your hand when crossing the street, but by the time this child is fifteen, this is no longer a reasonable expectation. Rules also vary with family circumstances. In some families, everyone is expected to eat at the same time, while in others, the eating schedule varies. A universal set of rules for all children does not exist. Your rules will depend on your values as well as on the needs and circumstances of your own particular family.

WHY HAVE RULES?

The first step in figuring out how to choose rules is to understand why we are bothering to have them. Here are some solid reasons.

For Physical Health

Sometimes rules are necessary to protect people's health. Parents may choose to limit their children's intake of sweets and junk food out of concern for their children's health. While one child may enjoy burning incense, if another is allergic to the smoke, then incense burning may not be allowed indoors. Loud music may not bother children, but if it gives their parents a headache or is a threat to the children's hearing, it should be turned down. All children need a minimal amount of sleep each night. Bedtimes should be set, but according to the age and needs of the child. In general, younger children need more sleep than older children. Sleep needs also vary with the physical makeup and stamina of the child.

For Mental Health

Some rules can protect the mental health of our children. One example would be the restriction of video games to those which are nonviolent. Requiring that televisions, VCRs, and computers be confined to public spaces in the home can reduce antisocial, isolationist tendencies in some children.

For Safety

Limits can also be set in the name of safety. Jumping on beds can be dangerous. Books and toys on the floor can trip someone. Young children can get cut by sharp knives. Driving too fast can cause an accident.

To Protect Property

Limits can be set to protect property. If a compact disc is not returned to its case, it might get scratched. Walls can be ruined when written on with crayons. Puddles of water on the bathroom floor can rot the floor. Library books can be lost if not kept in a special place.

For Living in Harmony

Limits can also be set for the sake of peaceful relations among everyone in the house. If a bathroom has to be shared by several family members, then time limits can be set for each person. If music disturbs someone who has gone to bed, then it should be turned down. Permission should be asked before you borrow someone else's possession. Everyone has the right to be involved in family conversations, even the youngest child, who may not be as eloquent.

Moral and Religious Values

One parent may consider bad language to be crude and repulsive while another may view its occasional use as a harmless release of tension. One parent may consider attendance at weekly religious services to be an absolute while another may never attend services. Only you can decide which rules are meaningful for your family.

CHOOSING YOUR RULES

Take a few minutes to jot down the rules you think are important for your family. Then place them into the following categories:

Protect health of child or others

Protect safety of child or others

Protect rights of others

Protect property

Encourage cooperative living

Uphold moral or religious values

Other

In choosing our rules, we must be sure that they C.A.N. be successful: that they are Clear, Appropriate, and Necessary.

Clear

We need to spell out clearly for our children just what it is that we expect of them. "Don't be home late" will not work with children. What is late to us may be early to them. It's always safest to specify the time we want them to be home.

Whenever possible, our rules should be stated in the affirmative: "do" rather than "don't." Expressing rules in terms of the behaviors we expect (e.g., use the crayons on paper) rather than in terms of those we do not want to see (e.g., don't use crayons on the wall) sends children a clear message about how to act. Often when we tell children "do not," they seem to have selective hearing. They hear the "do" but not the "not" or they may hear only the end of the sentence and not the beginning. What do you think the first thing a young child who is told "Don't put beans in your nose" will do?

Appropriate

It's helpful to examine our rules as our children grow. The limits we set for our children will change as our needs and our children's needs change. When our children are younger, we may have to restrict them to playing in the yard. The older they get, the farther they can venture from home. A six-year-old should not use the food processor, but a sixteen-year-old might. Ideally, as our children get older, they can assume more responsibility for themselves and need fewer limits. For example, bedtimes get later as children get older. By the time they are in high school, they can set their own bedtimes. Ironically, as our children get older, we often give them harsher rules than when they were younger. Relaxing and changing our limits as our children mature presents a difficult challenge to many parents. It's hard to let go.

Necessary

Look at the rules in each category listed above. We should ask ourselves: "How important is this rule to me? Do I have a really good reason for sticking with it?" Be sure that your limits really matter to you and that they are truly worth upholding. Take particular note of those in the last category. Do you really need them? The fewer rules or limits, the better. The more you have, the harder it will be for your children to remember them. If you spend too much time trying to enforce low-priority rules, you may be winning a lot of little battles and losing the war.

Often we do not realize the need for a rule until we are faced with a problem. One day, my seven-year-old daughter went straight from school to her friend's house. It never occurred to her that she should tell me first since she often went to this friend's house to play after she came home and had her snack. After spending many anxious minutes tracking her down, I realized that I had never told her to check with me first.

HOW TO GET YOUR KIDS TO OBEY THE RULES

Give Kids a Voice

Kids need a voice in setting limits. They need a chance to tell you what they think and feel. Even a child of five or six can talk with you and help you set fair limits. When kids help you make rules, they are more likely to obey them. However, listening to them does not mean that you necessarily have to agree with them enough to change your rules. Some limits can be set together and some have to be set by you alone.

Tell Them Why

Children are more likely to obey rules when they know the reasons behind them. "You cannot take your bike across town because I said so" is a rule with no explanation. "You cannot take your bike across town because there is too much traffic and you might get hurt" includes an explanation with the rule. While your child may not agree with you, your child can certainly understand your reasoning. Put yourself in your child's position. How would you feel if someone forbade you from taking a hike in a park but didn't tell you why? Knowing that behind every rule lies a reason that makes sense makes it much more likely that you will obey the rule.

Give Them Advance Warning

Try not to spring rules on your children all of a sudden. Let your children know about the rule before they break it. How is a child supposed to know not to ride her bike into town unless you have told her in advance? The child should know early on how far from home she may ride her bike. As she grows older, together you can discuss lengthening this distance.

Give Them Reminders

Children sometimes forget rules. So do adults. If you see that your child may have forgotten a limit, don't wait until he's in trouble; gently remind him now. But if your child forgets more than two or three times and your reminding turns into nagging, stop reminding and follow through with consequences.

Say What You Mean

Be very clear about your limits. Think through what you mean and give specific, clear directions. Children need to hear exactly what behavior you expect. General instructions may mean something totally different to your child than to you. A teenager who is told to be home "not too late" may return home at two A.M. to a frantic parent. "Not too late" often has a totally different meaning to a child than to a parent. "Be home by midnight" makes your expectations clear.

Be Positive Whenever Possible

Whenever you can, try to have your rules be "dos" instead of "don'ts." "Dos" are more encouraging. They let the child clearly understand correct behavior. "You can play with balls outside" instead of "Don't play with balls inside." Or "Wash your hands before coming to the table" instead of "Don't come to the table with dirty hands." "Don'ts" are sometimes a temptation—they may even put ideas in a child's head. Craig never thought of putting beans in his nose until his mother told him, "Don't put beans up your nose."

All children need limits to help them grow up to be safe, healthy, well-adjusted people. Getting children to obey rules can be challenging and frustrating at times. But there is much we can do to make this job easier. Understanding why we have rules and explaining our reasons to our children, keeping an open mind, giving children a say, being clear, and being positive whenever possible set the stage for good discipline.

SUMMARY OF MAIN POINTS

◆ Children need limits that give them safety and security as well as the freedom to enjoy life.

◆ When rules are unreasonable, children react with blind obedience, stubbornness, and sneakiness.

◆ When no rules exist, children react with impulsivity, fear, risk-taking behavior, and feel feelings of rejection.

◆ When rules are fair and meaningful, children feel secure and are more likely to comply.

◆ Protection of health, safety, property, harmonious living, and moral and religious values are sound reasons for having rules.

◆ Children are more likely to obey rules if they have a say in making them.

◆ Children are more likely to obey rules if they understand the reasons behind the rules.

• Children are more likely to obey rules if they are informed about them and reminded periodically.

• Children are more likely to obey rules if the rules are stated clearly.

• Children are more likely to obey rules if the rules are framed positively.

CHAPTER FOUR

Encouragement, Praise, and Rewards

Positive feedback can provide children with the encouragement that inspires them to behave appropriately. It can give them the courage to put their best foot forward, the courage to assume responsibility for their own actions, and the courage to face life and its challenges. Having positive expectations, praising, and rewarding appropriate behavior are all tools of encouragement, but if misused, they can become tools of discouragement. Let's look at how we can use positive expectations, praise, and rewards to provide the encouragement our children need to behave appropriately.

EXPECTING THE POSITIVE

Isn't it a wonderful feeling when we know that someone has confidence that we'll succeed! "This is challenging, but I think you can handle it," "I expect that you'll follow through with your promise," and "I'm sure you'll take care of it" are messages of our confidence in our children's abilities. These are words of encouragement that propel our children in the direction of appropriate behavior. If we let our children know that we have confidence that they will do the right thing rather than threatening them lest they do the wrong thing, our children will be more likely to behave appropriately. Our words can become self-fulfilling prophecies for our children. They will often deliver what we predict they will deliver.

Certainly, just because we have positive expectations does not mean that children will always behave as we wish. No matter how encouraging and positive we are, children will still misbehave. Making mistakes is an essential part of figuring out how to get along in this world. But at least our positive and appropriate expectations set them off in the right direction. Most children do want to please us and will try harder to live up to our expectations if they think we believe they can. I wonder if "I think I can, I think I can" would ever have entered the mind of the Little Engine That Could if the older engine had not already given him the message that "*I* think you can."

Here are some helpful questions to ask ourselves to help us encourage our children with positive expectations:

* Do I really believe that my children can and will live up to my expectations?

* Do I let them know that I have confidence in them?

* Do I threaten (implying that I will meet with resistance), "If you don't, then————" or do I promise (implying that I expect cooperation), "When you do, then————"

PRAISING

As parents, we are constantly bombarded by "experts" who tell us that we need to praise our children more. "Praise them and they'll obey you." "Praise them and they'll have high self-esteem." "Praise them and they'll be more successful in school." Yes, praise can encourage children and give them that lift that inspires them to continue in a positive direction. But not all praise is encouraging. In fact, some praise is downright discouraging and may even push children in the direction of misbehavior. Sometimes praise can backfire on us and actually steer our children away from meeting our expectations if it is insincere, overly effusive, or manipulative.

Every single person on this earth, and especially a child, needs praise. Hearing good things about ourselves can make us feel good and motivate us to want to succeed and act appropriately. Praise has two parts to it. The first part is the words we actually speak. The second part is the one that really counts—the child's translation or interpretation of those words (Ginott, *Between Parent and Child*, 1976). Does the child interpret the praise to mean that he is capable and competent, or does the child feel unworthy and undeserving as a result of the praise?

How can we parents develop the skill of providing encouraging praise to our children, praise that can give them fuel to continue along a successful path? Here are some basic guidelines that can help assure that our praise achieves its intended purpose.

Guidelines

Remember to notice the positive, be it ever so slight.

Mrs. G. comes home exhausted from work and sees coats and books all over the den. "Why have you left such a mess here? Why don't you ever clean up after yourselves?" But what she failed to notice was that all the breakfast dishes were done and the dinner table was set. Sometimes, as parents, it is easy to forget to notice what our children are doing right. We zero in on what must be corrected. But we must try to remember to let our children know what they are doing right as well as the mistakes they make. Remember, when they are changing their behavior, tell them how well they are doing, even if they improved just a little. Even though the rest of the room may be a mess, you can notice, "Great, you cleaned up your closet." A good rule of thumb is to try to give two positive, sincere comments for every time you correct them.

Mean what you say.

Did you ever run to the store for a last-minute item, feeling bedraggled and unkempt, hoping no one would see you? And then, just as you're about to slink out the door, someone you haven't seen in a while calls out your name. Hesitantly you approach and the person exclaims how marvelous you look. How did it make you feel? Chances are one of these thoughts passed through your mind. "Wow, I *really* must have looked horrible before" or "What a phony person—I can't believe a thing this person says" or "Why is s/he saying this, what does s/he want from me?" Perhaps the praise was well intentioned, but it sure didn't make you feel very good.

How does it feel when someone tells you that you did a great job when you know that you didn't? Discouraged from improving since the minimal effort seems to satisfy the person? Embarrassed or down on yourself because you know the person feels sorry for you and therefore gave you a compliment? Mistrustful of that person because he was dishonest? Disrespectful of that person's judgment? Wondering what that person wants from you?

Now let's look at this from the child's point of view. Dishonest praise discourages children. The intentions of the praiser do not matter. What matters is how the child feels as a result of the praise. If a child figures out (and children are *very* perceptive) that the praiser is just trying to make him feel good, then he may feel worse. "Gee, I must be pretty pathetic if you feel you have to praise me so much to make me feel good." If it's praise for mediocrity with the hope that the praise will motivate them to do better, children often end up feeling worse than before and distrust parents or adults even when they praise them for real. "You told me my book report was wonderful and I got a C on it. How do I know you're being honest this time?" We may even believe our praise, but if our children suspect that our evaluations of them are totally biased, then they very likely might stop listening to us. "You're just saying that because you're my mother."

Insincere, manipulative praise often does not achieve its desired goal. A comment like "You threw the ball great" given to a child whose throwing is mediocre is unlikely to inspire greater throwing prowess. Embarrassment and discouragement are more likely outcomes. Instead, try to find an aspect where you can be honest in your praise—perhaps about their diligence or improvement. Before you praise, ask yourself, do I really mean it? If you don't mean it, don't say it!

Focus on the deed, not the doer.

When Jake shared his candy with his sister, his mother exclaimed, "Oh, Jake, you're such a good boy!" Yes, that was very kind of him to share his candy, but let's beware of overgeneralizing. What does it mean to be a "good boy" or a "good girl"? These terms give children nothing specific to hold on to to help them feel good about themselves. To kids, these terms sound like "good egg" or "bad egg," and they often lead to poor self-concepts. But if instead we say, "That was generous of you to share with your sister," then we are being honest and realistic, and Jake will have a satisfied feeling.

When praising, it's best to stick to the issue, and not cover the child's whole personality in one fell swoop. Stay focused on the deed, what the child did, rather than the doer, namely, the child. When Megan cleans her room, say, "This room looks sparkling clean" rather than "What a good girl you are for cleaning your room. You're such a neat little girl." When Justin admits that he broke the vase, say, "I appreciate that you told me" rather than "It's so wonderful that you were honest. I can always trust you." When Stephanie draws a picture say, "Those are interesting trees" or "The picture is very colorful" rather than "You're a wonderful artist." Children are encouraged by praise that lets them know specifically what they are doing right.

Turn the pride back to the child.

Picture a child running in exclaiming, "We won, we won the game!" Our first instinct would probably be to say, "I'm so proud of you!" Our praise focuses on ourselves. Wouldn't he feel even better if instead our praise helped him focus on himself? "You must feel so proud of your win." When a child gets 100 on a test, the comment "You must feel so good. You worked so hard" gives a child more joy than "I'm so proud of you." Turning the pride back to the child is a way to encourage the child to praise and feel good about himself.

Stick to one person and avoid comparison.

Praise should be given in its own right, not as a way to manipulate children to behave or achieve. Mom walks into the room. Matt, Tom, and Liz are running around. Courtney is sitting quietly at a table doing a puzzle. "I like the way Courtney is playing so quietly!" exclaims Mother. What's going on? Mom is praising Courtney to get all the other children to settle down. Mom certainly means well. But the best-laid plans often do go astray. In a case like this, the one praised often feels "used" and the other children often feel resentful. We can just imagine what might be going through Matt, Tom, and Liz's minds—"Boy, that Courtney! What a Goody Two-Shoes. I can hardly wait to get back at her." Unfortunately, none of the children is helped by this form of praise, even if they do settle down for a few minutes.

When praise involves a comparison to others, children can be discouraged. "You're the best in the family in math." "I wish I could depend on your brother and sister the way I can depend on you." What a burden to place on a child! How can he ever live up to all this praise?

What happens when one child is praised at the other's expense?

"You draw much better than your sister." "Unlike your brother, you did a nice job cleaning up your room." Comparative praise like this only makes kids resentful of each other. Often the praised child feels guilty and uncomfortable ("Gee, I know my brother worked harder than I did") or worse, gloats about it ("Ha, ha, I'm better than you are!"). The other child may feel rejected, defeated, and resentful of the child being praised, and may very well take it out on the sibling when the parents are not around. Sibling rivalry and hostility thrive and flourish under this kind of praise.

When we make comparisons, we are treading on very dangerous ground. We discussed previously how children do as we do. We may find comparative praise thrown right back in our faces. Children may learn how to get one parent to do something by praising the other parent. "Mom is nice. She lets me watch TV." "Dad's so generous. He always buys me a treat at the store." This gets even worse when parents are divorced and children learn to use this technique on the parent they are with at the time. "Dad is so much fun. He takes me to the movies." Children learn very quickly how to use this form of comparative praise to stir up their parents' competitive "juices" and get what they want. "You're much nicer than Mom; she never takes me to the movies." "I like going to Daddy's better than staying here. He buys me lots of presents." Imagine how hurt and angry Mom would be upon hearing that. A good rule of thumb: praise without comparisons.

Cool it—praise can be addictive.

Five-year-old Leslie received quite a shock when she entered kindergarten. All her life she had been told by her parents that she was the smartest, prettiest, most talented little girl. And, lo and behold, she enters kindergarten and she meets a whole class full of smart, talented children. Yes, she can tie her shoes, draw pretty pictures, and spell her name, but so can her friends. What happens? Leslie starts to feel insecure; something is missing. When the compliments she awaits do not surface, Leslie may come home from school complaining, "The teacher doesn't like me. She didn't even notice my beautiful dress."

Praise can discourage us and rob us of our desire to keep trying. It can thwart us from meeting life's challenges. It can even make us feel bad about ourselves. Just as flies can drown in too much honey, children can drown in too much praise. What happens to the little girl who has been told, "You're the most beautiful child in the whole world. Your teacher is going to think you're so pretty" when she gets to school and there's a whole classroom full of pretty children?

Too much of anything is not good. Too much praise can be just as harmful as not enough praise. Sometimes when we praise our children too much, we are setting them up for disappointment. They develop unrealistic expectations for themselves that are unlikely to be met, as with Leslie. They become confused. "Why didn't the teacher like me? Why didn't all the kids play with me?" Then they feel bad about themselves. They feel that they should be that good, that their parents expect them to be that good, and, therefore, they are letting themselves and their parents down.

When we praise too much, we create praise "junkies," children who cannot function without massive doses of praise. Self-control is beyond their realm—they are controlled by praise. Praise "fixes" motivate them to succeed or to conform. They often will perform only when someone notices them. If the report won't be graded, they'll put in a minimal effort. If no one is around to compliment them on their neatness, they'll throw trash on the ground.

Tone it down.

Praise can be burdensome. At a family gathering, Rachel's mother raved about the way Rachel played with her little sister. Suddenly, Rachel began hitting her cousin and throwing blocks around. How did that lovely little angel suddenly turn into a monster?

Sometimes when we praise too much, we actually encourage misbehavior. When some children are lavishly complimented, they feel guilty and undeserving. Sure, they may have helped clean the house, but at the same time they may have wished their brother broke his leg. They misbehave just to set things straight, to be sure that no one expects too much of them. Also, sometimes too much praise makes children feel so powerful that they think they can do anything they want.

Many children feel weighted down by the burden of too much praise. How can they ever live up to it? What happens if they mess up? They, too, may choose to misbehave just to remove that heavy load from their shoulders.

Summary

Praise is one tool we parents use to encourage our children to behave appropriately. Honest, sincere praise that is not manipulative and stays focused on both the issue and the child can be a great source of encouragement.

REWARDING

We can also use rewards to help us set the stage for our children to behave appropriately and to minimize discipline problems. The rationale behind using rewards as a discipline tool is that when an action is followed by a reward or a payoff, the action is more likely to be repeated. Thus, the thinking goes, if children receive rewards for appropriate behavior, they will be more likely to continue that same behavior. Rewards are considered to be a positive way to motivate kids to do what we want them to, especially at times when they wouldn't ordinarily do it on their own. "If you vacuum the house, I'll lend you my car"; "After you finish your work, you can have a piece of candy"; "When your teeth are brushed, you can watch television." "You washed the car so beautifully, why don't you take it for a spin."

Parent A who states, "I'll take you out to dinner if you clean your room" and Parent B who states, "Wow, you cleaned your room so well, let's celebrate and go out to dinner" are both rewarding their children for cleaning their rooms. But what is the difference between them? They are using two different kinds of reward strategies. Parent A is using a planned reward, a reward that is promised to the child ahead of time on the condition that he does what he is asked. Parent B is using a spontaneous reward, a reward that is unexpected and comes after the behavior; no conditions for the reward have been set ahead of time, and the child does not know in advance that it will be received. Both planned and spontaneous rewards can have a role in teaching discipline. Both can be positive discipline tools . . . sometimes.

Planned Rewards

Mother promised Jim a new CD if he kept his room clean for a week. Dad promised the boys $5 for each A they got on their report card. Mrs. T. promised Brandon a sticker for every day he dressed himself. Mrs. M. promised Jessica a new doll if she didn't wet her training pants. Mr. S. promised his son a new baseball cap if he didn't use any bad words for two weeks. The CD, the money, the sticker, the doll, and the baseball cap are all planned rewards; they were promised ahead of time to be given if the condition was met—that the child behaved the way the adult wanted.

Before discussing how planned rewards can be used in teaching discipline, it is important to first be aware of some of the problems that can arise when planned rewards are used.

Rewards can become addictive. Just as addicts need to increase their dosages to get the same high, so, too, do many children need more and bigger rewards to motivate them to behave appropriately. "I don't want just one piece of candy for cleaning my room. I cleaned it really well. Why can't I have two pieces of candy?" "I have lots of stickers. I want bigger stickers now." "I'm saving for a stereo. I need five dollars when I pick up my clothes." "Teacher, I worked really hard on that assignment. Can't I have two smiley faces instead of one?" "Give me more, more, more" becomes the theme song of some children when planned rewards are used as a major approach for disciplining them.

Planned rewards can become habit-forming. Parents like using them because they are easy to think up and the parents can see some results right away. However, too much of anything is not good. No matter how much we may like ice cream, if we have it several times a day every single day, we will probably get tired of it. The more you use rewards, the less they work because they become less and less meaningful to the children. "Who cares?" becomes their response to a promise of a reward.

Planned rewards often result in children taking on a very selfish approach of "I'll do it only if it benefits me." Brad's Mom told him she was having company and she would like him to take out the trash. She promised him his usual dollar for doing this chore. "Sorry, Mom, I'm busy right now, and besides I don't need the money. I have plenty of cash right now." As the words "Do——— and I'll———; I'll give you———if you———; If you do———, I'll pay you———" start cropping up more and more in parents' conversations with their children, the children develop their own pet phrases: "Whatcha gonna give me?" and "What's in it for me?" Children start to lose sight of the fact that all of us have to have self-control and behave appropriately because we all share this earth together.

Too many rewards end up robbing children of the desire to do something because they know inside it's the right thing to do. Some excessively rewarded children are only nice to people they think can help them; they keep their own space clean but have no respect for public spaces; and they only read a book if they are getting school credit for it.

Children are great mimics. They know how to act just like us. "I'll stop fighting if you buy me those new tennis shoes." "I'll do the dishes if you buy me some ice cream." Soon they start trying to get us to behave the way they think is appropriate by promising us rewards if we behave the way *they* want *us* to. "Thanks for the idea" is what they tell us when they try to promise us rewards in return.

A cardinal rule of parenting is *never say never*. Despite all these reservations, planned rewards can have their place in teaching children discipline. (With extremely disturbed or discouraged children, rewards may play a greater role. This book is not designed for children with severe behavior problems, although many of our suggestions will also work in those cases.) Planned rewards are most effective when they are used occasionally for a specific behavior problem, such as a bad habit, that can't seem to be solved any other way. The key to this approach is eventually to get the child to behave appropriately automatically, without needing a reward. At first, every time the child behaves appropriately, he must be consistently rewarded. After a period of rewarding every single time the child behaves appropriately, the reward should be given less frequently, such as perhaps after a week of appropriate behavior and then later on after a month, until gradually the rewards become farther and farther apart, and the child behaves appropriately automatically without thought of a reward.

Mr. T. gave Daniel a sticker each day he didn't pull the cat's tail. After Daniel started getting stickers every day in a row for two weeks, Mr. T. promised his son a toy car if he consistently did not pull the cat's tail for a week. After giving Daniel three little cars, Mr. T. promised him a garage for the cars if he did not pull the cat's tail for a month. By the end, Daniel had stopped pulling the cat's tail.

Many parents find charts helpful when they use a reward system. On the chart they keep a tally and record each time the child exhibits the behavior they are trying to encourage or doesn't exhibit the behavior they're trying to discourage. Perhaps the child gets a sticker or a check on the chart. After so many stickers or checks, the child then receives a reward. The visual chart helps a child to keep track of his progress. Young children sometimes consider the sticker itself to be a reward.

A note of caution. Be careful in choosing your rewards. The kind of reward should depend on the particular circumstances—the age of the child, what is meaningful to the child, the interest of the parents. Some rewards have problems built into them. Using money as a reward teaches children that they can try to pay people to do what they want them to do. "I'll give you five dollars to write the paper for me." Using food can create eating problems, especially with sweets. "Don't cry, have a cookie" has taught many young children to resort to food to solve their problems, only to develop eating disorders as adults.

When choosing a reward, try to find one that makes sense to the child, that's logically connected to the behavior you are trying to encourage. A new book rather than money makes much more sense for a good report card. A new game (particularly the new cooperative games that are on the market) works well for not fighting. Hearing a story after teeth are brushed, having time to relax after homework is done, borrowing the car after carpooling a younger sibling are all rewards that make sense. Some chores and deeds have their own rewards built into them. "If you brush your teeth, you will have fewer cavities." "If you clean your room, you will be able to find what you need." "If you read, you will enter a world of excitement and adventure." Others have secondary rewards. "If you help me with the laundry, I'll have time to take you to the mall."

Spontaneous Rewards

"Everyone pitched in so well cleaning today, let's go out to dinner." "It's the end of the semester; let's go out to celebrate." "We've worked so hard today, let's take a break and go to the movies." These are spontaneous rewards. These rewards are given after the fact without the terms for the reward being stated ahead of time.

Rather than promising our children rewards ahead of time to get them to do what we want, we can rejoice with them when they succeed. We can motivate our children to behave appropriately by celebrating their accomplishments with them. Children receive the message that we genuinely care about them, that we appreciate their effort, and that we are sharing with them rather than ruling them. Celebrations over accomplishments create a strong bond between parents and children.

Our American culture places far too much emphasis on competition and winning. Even when children lose a game or experience another disappointment, celebrations may be very important. "That was a great game even though you lost. Let's go out for pizza."

Our family has chosen an alternative to rewarding children for grades. We have a custom of going out for a report card dinner after report cards are sent home. The dinner is meant to be a celebration of an accomplishment, in this case, the end of the quarter. Attending the dinner does not depend on grades received.

Celebration over accomplishments inspires a cooperative atmosphere. Children feel that their parents are working together with them rather than working against them or trying to control them. This is a much more positive arena in which discipline can take place.

Summary

Each family must decide for itself the right balance between rewards and alternative discipline approaches, and between planned and spontaneous rewards. Some guiding questions that can help you decide which approach to take are:

✦ Does this reward make sense to my child? Is it related to what I want my child to do?

✦ What message am I sending to my child by offering this reward? "I care about you, I want to help you by giving you an incentive," or "I'm trying to bribe you because I'm desperate"?

✦ Does this reward encourage long-term behavior change?

✦ Will my child eventually be able to behave appropriately without a reward?

✦ What values am I teaching my child?

SUMMARY OF MAIN POINTS

✦ Positive expectations launch children in the direction of appropriate behavior.

✦ Honest, sincere, noncomparative praise given freely but not effusively can encourage appropriate behavior.

✦ Rewards can sometimes be effective discipline tools for correcting inappropriate behavior and motivating appropriate behavior.

✦ Rewards should be used thoughtfully and sparingly.

✦ Excessive use of rewards and comparative praise can backfire and create discipline problems.

CHAPTER FIVE

Talking and Listening

The way we communicate with our children is often the determining factor in how well they obey and respect us. Talking and listening to our children in ways that win them over to our side are communication skills we can develop with a little practice.

TALKING

The words we choose to let our children know our expectations and the words we choose to let them know when they have not lived up to these expectations can have a vital impact on our children's behavior. Our words can encourage or discourage appropriate behavior. Our words can enlist their cooperation or incite their rebellion.

Talking About Expectations: The Positive Approach

Sometimes it seems as if all we are doing is telling our children what not to do. "Don't touch the baby." "Don't go into the street." "Don't eat cookies before dinner." "Don't eat too much junk food." "Don't drink and drive." "No, you can't stay at the party longer." "No, you can't go to the movies today." All these negatives sure take a toll on us parents! They can really get us down. They can really get our kids down, too.

Honey draws more flies than vinegar. Often, with a little fore-thought, we can sweeten up our words, taking out the "nos" and still getting the same message across. Many of our negatives can be turned around and restated positively. Instead of saying "no" and "don't," we can provide alternatives or acceptable choices and emphasize what the child can do instead of what he/she cannot do. Doing this may take some practice. It's a challenge, but we can do it.

Example #1.

Picture yourself coming home after a hectic day—at work, running errands, or carpooling children. It's five minutes before the family's usual dinnertime. You frantically begin to prepare supper. Hungry children start rummaging through the cabinets looking for something to eat. Aha—they spy the cookies. Your first impulse would probably be to yell out, "Don't eat cookies before dinner. They'll spoil your appetite." How could you transform this message from a negative to a positive one? Some possibilities:

Would you like to have your salad before dinner or wait?

Find a piece of fruit or a vegetable to eat now. You can set the cookie aside for dessert.

I'm sure you're hungry. Find a healthy snack to tide you over. You can have the cookie after supper.

A cookie will spoil your appetite. Find something healthy to eat now and save the cookie for dessert.

What are other possible words Mom could have used?

Example #2.

When teens get their driver's licenses, they have a newfound sense of freedom. Far-flung friends now seem to be within their reach. Not long after she received her driver's license, our daughter declared that she would like to drive to visit her friends in Atlanta, a distance of approximately seventy miles, some on country roads, some on major highways. Our first instinct was to declare, "No, way! You can't drive that far!" What might be some alternative answers that would not have been so negative, that would not have cut her right off?

Let's go to Atlanta together a few times with you driving. Then, when you've had more experience, you can drive on your own.

That would be fine after you have had several months' experience driving around our town.

Atlanta has more traffic than our town, and the highways are sometimes confusing. It's important for you to practice with us in the car guiding you before you do it on your own.

What other positive approaches could we parents have taken in this situation?

Example #3.

Three-year-old Felicia was quite curious about her new baby brother. While he was sleeping, she stuck her hand through the bars of the crib and explored his little fingers and hand. The baby, startled, began to cry. Upon seeing Felicia at the side of the crib, Mother's first instinct was to exclaim, "Don't touch the baby." Then, Felicia began to cry. "Why is everyone paying attention to the baby? What's so special about him? I don't like this baby at all.

He gets me into trouble." What other approach could Mother have taken?

> *You're curious about the baby. But babies are fragile and can get hurt if we don't handle them properly.*
>
> or
>
> *The baby is sleeping now. Touching him will disturb him. You can play with him when he wakes up.*

Just a sample of possible positive answers has been provided for these two situations. Ask yourself, "Is there something else that would be appealing for my child to do instead? How could I tactfully suggest this alternative?" With practice, you will be able to come up with many other ways to tell your children what they can do rather than what they can't do. The "honey" approach, giving a positive rather than a negative message, may seem a bit like artificial sweetener at first, but with practice it will come naturally. If children have become used to hearing nothing but "no," they may not pay attention to the positive approach at first. But don't be discouraged; keep it up, and they'll catch on eventually.

A note of caution. We have to be careful that we offer our children choices only when we can accept the choice they make. When asked, "Will you pick the book up?" a child has a choice of answering either yes or no, even though we really don't mean to offer that choice. We want the child to pick the book up. "Please pick up the book" is a positive (or at least kind), yet firm way of getting the task accomplished. "Will you take out the trash?" allows the child the option of saying "No, I don't want to take out the trash" while "Please take out the trash" or "When will you take out the trash?" are polite, yet firm statements of an expectation. The bottom line—don't word a request "Will you" if you can't accept "I won't" as an answer.

Talking About Expectations: When the Positive Approach Won't Work

Positive verbal approaches do not always work. Sometimes our children want to do something that we cannot allow them to do and we cannot find alternative choices. But rather than just say no, a helpful approach in getting them to cooperate with us is to (1) explain our reasons for saying no, (2) acknowledge our children's feelings of disappointment, (3) say it kindly. We can firmly say "no" while still being kind to them and sensitive to their disappointment or anger. Saying no is indeed harder than taking the positive approach, but there are times when we have no other choice.

Example #4.

Five-year-old Darrell is having a terrific time at his friend's birthday party. They've played pin the tail on the donkey, eaten cake and ice cream, opened presents, and now he and his friends are playing tag. What excitement! Meanwhile, Mom is beginning to get anxious. It's already four-thirty. She must leave now to avoid rush-hour traffic. She has an important meeting at six-thirty.

> MOM: *We can't stay at the party any longer, Darrell. We have to go now.*
> DARRELL: *But, Mom, I'm having such a good time.*
> MOM: *I said we have to go.*
> DARRELL: *But, Mom . . .*
> MOM: *Come with me right this minute, young man. We have to go.*

How could Mom have said no just as firmly but with more kindness, explaining her reason and acknowledging her child's disappointment? Here are some possible suggestions:

You'd like to stay at the party longer. You're having so much fun, but it's late and we have to be home for suppertime.

or

It's so much fun here. It's hard to leave, but we have to get home on time. We'll come back again.

or

You're having such a good time that it's hard to leave. I wish we could stay here, but I have to be home for my meeting.

How else might you have turned this situation around?

Example #5.

Teens love their independence and privacy. They also love parties, especially those without adult chaperons. Fifteen-year-old Suzanne approached her parents about having a party at her house—after her parents leave for the evening. "Absolutely not. Under no circumstances," races through their minds. How could they communicate this message less negatively?

We understand that having parents around would dampen the party. It may be embarrassing to you to have us there. But it is our responsibility to be home. We'll try to be as invisible as possible.

or

Adults can sure dampen a party, but we feel responsible for what happens in our house. It's our responsibility to be at home during the party.

or

You and your friends would feel more comfortable without adults around. We'll try to keep out of the way, but we have a responsibility to make sure nothing happens and that no one brings in alcohol.

What other responses might be appropriate?

As in these two cases, you, too, can come up with numerous other ways to get the same message across in a positive way: "I understand what you feel, but I cannot let you do what you want to and this is why. . . ." This way you are setting down limits without having to use negative expressions. By acknowledging our children's feelings and by making the effort to explain our reasons to them, we make them feel worthwhile, even if they are disappointed.

Sometimes parents try too hard to be positive with their children. Children are not so fragile that they cannot hear no sometimes. Don't be afraid to say no when it is necessary. Kids need to know their limits. When it comes to health and safety, our no has to come through loud and clear. But we can try to say no in the same respectful tone and spirit that we say yes.

Example #6.

Bobby, age ten, is jumping on the sofa.

MOM: *Bobby, floors are for jumping. Sofas are for sitting.*

BOBBY: *I know it, Mom, but I like to jump on the sofa. (He keeps jumping.)*

MOM: *Floors are for jumping. Sofas are for sitting.*

BOBBY: *The floor's too hard. I want to jump on something softer and springier. (He keeps jumping.)*

MOM: *You'd like to keep jumping on the sofa, but you could get hurt. Also, the sofa is an expensive piece of furniture and could break.*

BOBBY: *I'll be careful. Nothing will happen. (He keeps jumping.)*

What should Mom do? JUST SAY NO! "Stop jumping on the sofa right now." Mom needs to be more firm in her response. Kids need to know their limits. This is particularly important when it comes to computer use and movies. Sometimes it's in the best interest of our children to just say no.

Many of my student teachers have heard throughout their education courses how important it is to be positive with children. They have been repeatedly warned about the dangers of negative feedback. So when I, their supervising professor, come to observe them, they try to be as positive as possible—to the point where they are failing to teach the children right from wrong. A child will persist in misbehaving even after the teacher has tried to positively redirect him. Rather than say, "No, we can't do that here," the teacher will give up. Why? She doesn't want to be negative and discourage the child. What she doesn't realize is that sometimes children need that negative feedback. They need to be told when they have made a mistake. They need to be told directly not to do something again.

It's how we say no that matters. "No, you brat, stop it right now," or "Please stop that behavior right now. It's inappropriate"—the choice is ours. If a child has not responded to our positive redirection, then a clear but respectful no is in order.

Example #7.

Your child wants to ride his bike without wearing a helmet. He thinks helmets aren't cool. Since by not wearing a helmet, his physical safety is at risk, you need to say loudly and clearly, "It may feel funny wearing your helmet, but you cannot ride your bike without your helmet. You could get hurt." Then perhaps you could suggest ways to decorate the helmet so it will be more attractive or point out racers and their helmets.

Example #8.

Your fourteen-year-old wants to attend a high school party at someone's house, and the parents will be out of town. "You cannot attend the party unless an adult will be present" is a reasonable (but not popular) response.

Sometimes we just don't feel like we can accommodate our children's requests, and we don't want to bother with thinking up positive answers. Sometimes we may be angry at them and don't want to help them out. That's okay at times. We're only human. But we should try to say no in a way that is not sarcastic or humiliating.

Example #9.

Our child asks us to drive him and his friends to the movies. We have a million other things to do and feel quite hassled. You may be thinking, "No, you are so spoiled, always asking me to take you to the movies. Who do you think I am, your chauffeur?" But you can get your point across and still keep good relations between you and your child with answers like the following:

I'm quite busy today. I wish I had time to take you, and know it's disappointing not to go.

or

I'm sorry, but I have too much work to do around the house. I know how much you'd like to go—perhaps someone else can take you.

or

I have to——and——and——. By the time I finish, it will be too late to take you. I'm sorry. I know you were looking forward to going.

or

Since I had to take out the trash and do all the dishes, I don't have time to run to the mall. I'm sorry you're upset.

There are times when we choose to say no for our own personal reasons and other times when we feel obligated to say no. Questions that are helpful to ask ourselves on these occasions that can guide us in giving kind but firm responses are: What is my child feeling? How can I verbalize these feelings? Why can't my child do what s/he wants? How can I explain this to my child?

Talking About Feelings: We're Human, Too

Did you ever have a long, tiring day at work and come home to a house that looks like a tornado hit it? You're exhausted, you can barely keep your head up, and yet if you don't, you'll break your neck tripping over the jackets, toys, and books that are strewn in your path. You worked hard cleaning the house yesterday, and now look at it!

What might be your first reactions? Perhaps you might react with sarcasm: "What do you think I am, a slave?" or with insults: "You are the biggest slobs I have ever seen" or with threats: "If you don't clean this up right now, you're grounded for a year" or with punishments: "Look at this house. You can't have any friends over for one month!" Or you might try to make them suffer by giving them the "silent treatment" and acting as though they're invisible and that you are deaf to their words. Stop and think: What good will this do? Sarcasm and insults cut deeply, hurt children's self-esteem, and do not inspire them to rectify the damage. Threats and punishments place a burden upon you, forcing you to be the police officer who follows through on the threats and enforces the punishments. The silent treatment only generates more tension for all of you.

Actually, what we really want at times like these is to let our kids know how we feel—disappointed, shocked, put-upon—but we can't just yell this out. Let's look at how we can use an "I Message" to change their behavior. This approach has proved to work incredibly well to help children realize that what they have done affects us, to help them learn to respect our feelings, and to inspire them to change their behavior. Letting kids know how we feel, when we feel this way, and the reason we feel this way changes the whole picture. Instead of resenting us and our authority, they usually empathize with us. While resentment triggers rebellion, empathy inspires cooperation. Here's how to express how we feel with an "I message":

1. "When . . ."

Try to describe the situation that is upsetting you without pointing an accusatory finger at the child. This means describing what has happened but leaving out an accusatory or blaming "you" so that you don't put the child in a defensive rather than cooperative mode.

For example, say, "When there are books and clothes all over the floor" rather than "When you're such a slob." Or say, "When I'm studying and there's noise," rather than "You kids are so inconsiderate."

Using the word *when* helps narrow the problem to a specific time and thus gives the child hope that rectifying the behavior can be accomplished. Rather than expressing blanket disappointment in the child, such as "You never do things right" or "You always get it wrong," you are describing the specific situation that is bothersome and thus providing the child with hope that the solution is manageable.

2. "I feel . . ."

Try to express your feelings specifically and try to avoid using general words like *angry, mad,* and *upset.* Try to get at the emotion that lies at the heart of it all. Some suggested words are: *put-upon, frustrated, overwhelmed, insulted, betrayed, frightened, worried, concerned, anxious, disappointed.* Upon first glance, we may think that anger is our emotion, but if we probe deeper, we often find another emotion below the surface. Picture a mom back in school, studying for a test. Her children are laughing and playing loudly in the next room. Rather than yell at the children angrily about how inconsiderate they are, wouldn't it be more helpful for her to get at the source of her anger and express her concerns? "When I'm studying and there's noise, I can't concentrate and I'm afraid that I won't pass my exam." (The next step would be to solve the problem. Perhaps the children would decide to move or play a quiet game.) Putting the message in terms of "I feel" often makes children stand up and take notice.

With an "I message" it's important to talk about how you feel about that particular incident, not about many incidents in the past. If you say, "I'm sick and tired of reminding you," they're likely to think "There she goes again." But if you say, "When I come home and there is a mess in the den, I feel very disappointed," they can listen to your message and see that it makes sense without feeling put in a defensive position.

3. "Because . . ."

Let them know why you feel this way. Giving a reason helps them understand the origin of your feelings. In a sense, it justifies your right to these feelings and sells the message to them. "I feel put-upon when I come home and there are books and clothes all over the floor because then I have to clean them up and I'm exhausted." "When you come home late for supper, I feel disappointed because we don't get to eat together, and also I feel inconvenienced having to keep dinner warm."

What goes through kids' minds when they hear "I messages" such as these? Usually, they react with a thought such as "Gee, I'd better clean up. It really isn't fair." "I put the stuff there, I should clean it up." "I'll try to be on time for dinner. She enjoys my company."

We can also use the "I message" to express positive emotions and in that way encourage appropriate behavior. We come home from work, exhausted, dreading the thought of having to make dinner. We go into the kitchen and find the table set, food on the stove, and the sink clear. "I felt so relieved when I came home and dinner was ready because I am totally exhausted and didn't know how I would find the energy to prepare it." Imagine how terrific our children would feel! One response like this will inspire many other cooperative acts.

Labeling our feelings and explaining the reason for them does not just help us constructively get our problems off our chests but also helps our children get a clearer picture of the world around them. Children are very skillful at perceiving when we are upset, but often they do not understand why. If we do not explain the exact nature of our feelings and the reasons for them, then they might jump to their own conclusions. Their interpretations may be far more stressful to them than reality.

Example #10.

Mr. M. was very anxious when his children came home late, whether it was from school, from playing, or from a trip. His daughter Lynn assumed it was because her father didn't trust her. His son Joe assumed it was because he knew about something awful or dangerous and just wasn't telling him about it. The reality is that Mr. M. feels worried when someone is late because he remembers the trauma when he was a child, and his mother was once late because she was in a serious car accident. An "I message" would have been a tremendous benefit for both him and his children. "I am worried when someone is late because it reminds me of when my mom was late because she was in a serious car accident." This message helps him clarify his feelings and receive an empathetic response from his children.

Summary

Learning to express feelings constructively is a skill than can be mastered by adults and children alike with practice. The best time to practice is when you're calm, not in the middle of a heated argument. Starting with times when you feel good about something is often helpful. Remember to focus on expressing your feelings and describing the situation. By focusing on yourself and avoiding using the word *you* in an accusatory fashion whenever you can, you avoid blaming and putting the listener on the defensive. Your children will soon copy your "I messages." You can also directly teach them the three parts of the message and then practice some examples together.

One bonus when we use "I messages" is that our children learn to become more responsible for their actions. They learn that what they do affects others and that they can often rectify problems. An additional benefit is that when we have to compose an "I message" to fit a particular situation, it may take us a few minutes to think of what to say. These few moments may be just enough time to enable us to collect ourselves and calm down before we say or do anything we'll later regret.

LISTENING

Sometimes as parents it's hard for us to remember that communication means listening as well as talking. After all, we have so much to tell our children—so many rules, so many expectations, so many warnings—who has time to listen? But listen we must if we want them to listen to us. In fact, we should listen more than we talk. What's good for the goose is good for the gander.

Listening to children has important benefits. First, by listening, we will know what they are thinking and feeling. Second, if we listen, they will probably observe and imitate our listening behavior. Third, many discipline problems can be avoided if we don't jump to conclusions but rather take the time to listen to and hear the whole story.

How to Listen: Don't Jump to Conclusions

Listening means taking the time to hear a child out without jumping to premature conclusions. Look how Mom created problems by not listening.

MOM: *Why didn't you come right home from school, Dave? Where were you all this time?*

DAVE: *I went home with Josh because he—*

MOM: *That's nice. You went home with Josh while I was here worrying about you!*

DAVE: *I'm sorry, Mom, but Josh was—*

MOM: *Don't "but" me with your excuses. There's no reason why you had to go over to Josh's house instead of coming right home from school.*

DAVE: *I know, but, Mom—*

MOM: *Don't "but, Mom" me. You're not going to get away with this, young man. I'm going to ground you for a week.*

DAVE: *But, Mom, if only you—*

MOM: *There you go again with your "but, Mom." If I hear another "but, Mom," I'll ground you for a month. Now go up into your room until I tell you to come down.*

Unfortunately, Dave never got a chance to tell his mother that Josh got hurt at school and he took Josh home and stayed with him until his mother came home. Imagine Dave's frustration! Imagine his resentment toward his mother! Imagine his mother's embarrassment and guilt once she found out what happened!

We certainly can't blame Mom for being worried and anxious. Every horrible possibility probably ran through her mind while she was waiting for Dave. Look at how much easier it would have been for both of them if she had taken the time to hear him out and not jump to conclusions.

MOM: *Why didn't you come right home from school? Where were you all this time?*

DAVE: *I went home with Josh, Mom, because he got hurt at school and I had to stay with him until his mother came home.*

MOM: *I was worried sick.*

DAVE: *I'm sorry, Mom, I should have called you.*

MOM: *Dave, helping your friend was important. But it's also important to let me know what's going on so I won't worry.*

How to Listen: Give Your Undivided Attention

Sometimes we tell our children we are listening, but we are actually only listening with half an ear. We may be thinking about something else, busy with some other task, or just bored with what they have to say.

Jill tried to tell her mother about a serious problem she had in school. She had to follow her mother from one room to another, stop in the middle of sentences when the phone rang, and wait while her mother wrote a shopping list. How do you think Jill felt?

Mariah was explaining to her dad why she did not have a chance to finish her chores that day. Every time she paused to take a breath, he started to talk, and she had to remind him that she wasn't through. Dad just seemed to be anxiously waiting for her to get it all out so that he could finally say what was on his mind. Is that listening? Certainly not. Listening means paying attention to the words, not just superficially hearing them.

When our attention is divided, our children decide that we are not very interested in their ideas. Feeling unimportant, their self-esteem is lowered. They also learn from our example not to pay attention when others, including their parents, speak.

Our actions often speak louder than our words. We can be sure that our children know we are listening and focusing on them by allowing them time to express their thoughts and giving them feedback to let them know we heard them. Inserting an occasional "M-m-m," "I see," or "Okay" lets them know that we are listening.

How to Listen: Separate Yourself from Their Feelings

It's critical that when our children are upset and express their distress to us, we do not get sucked into their feelings and start to react in the same way. Try not to let their emotions get you worked up. Stay calm so that you can help them. Look what happened when Holly, age thirteen, comes home early from her friend's house.

MOM: *Oh, Holly, you're home early.*

HOLLY: *Yeah, Mom, I'm home. (grumpily)*

MOM: *You don't have to be so grouchy about it.*

HOLLY: *Who's grouchy?*

MOM: *You are, Holly. Just look at yourself. What a face! Have you forgotten how to smile lately?*

HOLLY: *What difference does that make?*

MOM: *It makes a lot of difference to me. I'm your mother and I refuse to put up with your bad moods. I just won't have it.*

HOLLY: *Well, I can't help it.*

MOM: *Of course you can help it. All you have to do is just pull yourself together and say, "I'm just not going to be grouchy anymore."*

HOLLY: *It's not that easy, Mom.*

MOM: *It is if you try.*

HOLLY: *TRY. TRY. TRY. That's all I hear day in and day out. You just don't understand.*

MOM: *No. I know, Holly. I never understand. You're the only one who understands anything. Too bad, isn't it, that you have such stupid parents.*

HOLLY: *Oh, Mom, don't start that, please. . . .*

MOM: *Start what? What am I starting? All I asked you is to try to be more cheerful. Now, is that asking too much of my own daughter?*

HOLLY: *Oh, Mom!*

MOM: *Stop that "Oh, Mom" stuff. Go right to your room, young lady, and don't come down until supper!*

What happened? Holly came home upset. Obviously, something happened outside the house that upset her. Holly's distress seemed to have nothing to do with Mom, yet Mom got defensive and acted as if it did. What could we suggest to Mom? Separate yourself.

It's pretty obvious when we see it on paper how this whole scenario could have been prevented. If only the mother had really listened to Holly's feelings and had picked up on them right away and acknowledged that she seemed upset, mother and daughter might not have gotten into a battle that ended up with a discipline problem. However, when we live these scenarios, it's not as obvious as when we read them. When our kids come home grumpy and on the attack, it's awfully hard not to get entwined in the tension and become a target.

When our kids get upset, it's easy for us parents to react defensively. But we get into trouble by taking their emotions personally and then trying to defend ourselves against them. Let them have their feelings. In fact, encourage them to have their feelings. The key is to S-E-P-A-R-A-T-E, look at them, listen to the feelings behind their words, and keep our own issues out.

How to Listen: Put Their Feelings into Words

An empathetically stated, "Gosh, you seem to be upset" would have been an entrée for Holly to start to put her feelings into words and talk to her mom about her concerns. If Mom incorrectly described these feelings, Holly would let her know and the discussion could continue. "No, I'm not upset. I'm mad." Holly's right to her feelings would be validated. She would see her mom as being there for her rather than as being opposed to her.

Have you ever been upset and someone tells you to cheer up, stop being upset? How did it make you feel? More upset or less upset? Usually, people end up feeling more upset—what a terrible put-down and insult! In addition to their first reason for feeling bad, they now have another reason—that their feelings don't matter to the other person. Picking up on and reflecting back the other person's feelings lets them know that they matter. "It sounds like you're really furious" or "You seem to be very nervous" or "It seems like you're insulted." If you've labeled the feeling incorrectly, they'll let you know. "No, I'm not furious, I'm scared."

Paying attention, separating, and labeling does not mean that you have to agree with the feelings. After hearing Holly's side of the story, Mom may have thought Holly was being petty with her friends. That doesn't matter. Mom's job is to be a sounding board, not a judge and jury. With the sounding board of a good listener, Holly can come to her own conclusions. When bad feelings come out, there's more room inside for the good feelings to take over. Let's look at how this approach could have worked for Holly and her mom:

MOM: *Oh, Holly, you're home early.*
HOLLY: *Yeah, I'm home. (grumpily)*
MOM: *You sound upset.*
HOLLY: *No, I'm angry.*
MOM: *You sound pretty mad.*
HOLLY: *Yeah, you wouldn't believe what happened.*
MOM: *What?*
HOLLY: *I was supposed to go to Amanda's house. Then Jane asked Amanda to go to the mall, so Amanda told me I couldn't come to her house.*
MOM: *So you felt hurt and rejected?*

HOLLY: *I sure did. I'll never make plans with Amanda again. She's such a fair-weather friend.*

MOM: *It sure is disappointing when something like that happens.*

HOLLY: *Yeah, it is. But I'll live. I've got a lot of work to do anyway.*

This time Mom's response put her in Holly's court. Mom didn't become the outlet for Holly's rage, and no fight erupted. Instead of making Holly feel worse, she helped her feel better by helping Holly express her own feelings and work her way through them.

Separating ourselves from our children's heated emotions and helping them put their feelings into words presents a great challenge to most of us when our kids attack us. "I hate you" or "You're the meanest parents in the world" or "You don't love me"—most of us parents have been victims of verbal onslaughts like these. How can they say that after all we've done for them! What should we do? Punish our children for talking that way? What good will it do? Punishing them for saying that they hate us will probably make them hate us even more. And this time they *really* feel their hate is justified.

It's okay to tell children that *hate* is a hurtful word that should not be used, but at the same time we can try to figure out and acknowledge their feelings. "You're really upset" or "You're really angry at me." Then if you can, try to get at the feeling that is masked by this rage. "You're frustrated by————," or "You're disappointed. You would have liked to————," or "You're sad about having to leave" or "You're embarrassed that————." Expressing the feelings in words teaches them to understand themselves and their reactions, and it shows them that you understand their feelings. They won't need to use the word *hate* if they can express what they are really feeling. Later, at a calm time, we can make it very clear that their behavior was inappropriate.

If we overreact to children's anger at us, get sucked up by their feelings, and don't help them verbalize their feelings, we can end up in serious battles that create major discipline headaches. Look what happened at the county fair:

AUSTIN: *Dad, please buy me some cotton candy.*
DAD: *It's too close to supper.*
AUSTIN: *Pleeeaaase. I never get a chance to have it.*
DAD: *I'm sorry, but it will spoil your appetite.*
AUSTIN: *You're the meanest dad in the world. I hate you.*
DAD: *Don't you dare talk to me that way!*
AUSTIN: *I can talk to you any way I want.*
DAD: *That's it! You're punished. We're leaving right now.*
AUSTIN: *But Dad—*
DAD: *Not another word out of you, or you won't ever go to a fair again.*

Look at what could have happened:

AUSTIN: *Dad, please buy me some cotton candy.*
DAD: *It's too close to supper.*
AUSTIN: *Pleeeaaase. I never get a chance to have it.*
DAD: *I'm sorry, but it will spoil your appetite.*
AUSTIN: *You're the meanest dad in the world. I hate you.*
DAD: *You're disappointed. That candy sure does look good.*
AUSTIN: *Yeah, I really want it.*
DAD: *It's hard to wait, but next time we come, we'll get it earlier in the day.*

In both cases, Austin did not get what he wanted. As a disciplinarian, the father was trying to set fair limits and stick to them. However, in the first case, both Dad and Austin ended up miserable, resentful of each other, and a discipline *issue* became a discipline *problem*. In the second case, discipline never turned into a problem. What was the difference? In the first case, the father focused on his own feelings rather than on his child's feelings and punished the child. In the second case the father separated himself from his child's feelings, listened, reflected, and put his child's feelings into words.

Is it proper for children to talk to their parents that way? Certainly not! But they do! And they will keep it up until we teach them other ways to articulate their feelings. These outbursts may still happen when our children get very angry, but they will be far less frequent if the outbursts go nowhere, as they did in the second scenario.

I've heard it said that children use tactics like name calling to manipulate their parents. Was Austin trying to manipulate his father by saying he hated him? Was he trying to make his father feel guilty and change his mind? Perhaps he was, but that does not matter. What matters is that the father stood firm and calm while at the same time acknowledging his child's right to his feelings.

Sometimes it would be nice to just wave a magic wand and take away our children's sad or unhappy feelings. We don't like to see their pain.

Debbie runs into her house breathless.

DEBBIE: *Mommy, Mommy, Karen's moving!*

MOMMY: *Yes. I know. Her mother told me.*

DEBBIE: *I don't want her to go. I want her to stay. If she leaves, I won't be able to play with her.*

MOMMY: *You'll find other friends. Another family will be moving into Karen's house. Perhaps they'll have a little girl your age.*

DEBBIE: *I don't want anyone else. I like Karen. I don't want her to move. Can we move too?*

MOMMY: *Don't be silly, Debbie. We can't do that. We're staying here.*

DEBBIE: *I wish I didn't have to. I want to go where Karen goes.* (crying)

MOMMY: *Now, stop that crying. Crying won't change things.*

Why don't you go out and ride your bike for a while?

DEBBIE: *I don't feel like riding my bike. I just feel like crying.*

MOMMY: *You're too big to cry. Stop!*

DEBBIE: *I can't stop. Every time I think of Karen, I feel sad.* (cries)

MOMMY: *How about watching TV for a while? That will get your mind off Karen.*

DEBBIE: *But when I watch TV I'll be thinking about Karen.* (crying continues)

MOMMY: *You're driving me crazy. Stop crying or I'll really give you something to cry about.*

How did the mother try to help Debbie?

Replace her friend with another ("You'll find other friends.")

Distract her ("How about watching TV for a while?")

Lecture to her ("Don't be silly, Debbie. We can't do that.")

Make her feel guilty ("You're driving me crazy.")

Instead, just by paying attention to Debbie, separating herself from the pain, and putting Debbie's feelings into words, the mother could have helped Debbie with her disappointment and prevented conflict between herself and her daughter:

DEBBIE: *Mommy, Mommy, Karen's moving.*

MOMMY: *Yes, I know. Her mother told me.*

DEBBIE: *I don't want her to go. I want her to stay. She's my friend. If she leaves, I won't be able to play with her.*

MOMMY: *You must be feeling very sad.*

DEBBIE: *Yes, I am. I'll miss her.*

MOMMY: *It's hard, honey, to see her go.*

DEBBIE: *Yes, it is.*

It might have been tempting for Mommy to tell Debbie that she'll make new friends, but that's not what Debbie needed at the time. She just needed someone to acknowledge her feelings.

Summary

The way we listen to our children can send either of two messages: "We really care about what you think and feel," or "We're not interested in what you think and feel." Like a boomerang, children will then send the very same message back to us that we send them. Some tips for listening so that we get our children on our side are:

1. Don't jump to conclusions. Hear them out. Give them enough time to speak, and wait until they are through before you say anything.

2. Pay attention when they speak. Stay focused on them. Don't try to do ten other things at the same time. Give them signs that you are listening: "I see" or "M-m-m" or "Okay" or "Yes."

3. Separate yourself from their feelings. Don't overreact and take their feelings personally. Try to stay focused on the issue and not on yourself.

4. Attach words to their feelings. Try to rephrase what you think they are feeling, but try to avoid mimicking their words. If you don't pinpoint the correct feeling, they'll let you know.

SUMMARY OF MAIN POINTS

• Talking and listening to our children are communication skills we can learn with practice.

• Sometimes we can express our expectations of our children positively. We can provide them with alternative choices and let them know what they can do rather than what they can't do.

• Sometimes a positive statement of expectations is not possible. Then we must kindly yet firmly say no.

• Children will be more likely to listen and obey our "nos" if we explain our reasons and acknowledge their feelings of disappointment.

• Three-part "I messages" ("I feel——when—— because——") let our children know that we have feelings, too. They also motivate children to change their behavior and be cooperative.

• Effective listening means hearing children out, giving them our undivided attention, separating ourselves from their emotions, and putting their feelings into words. Effective listening will help us avoid many discipline problems.

CHAPTER SIX

Harnessing Our Anger

It is perfectly normal that angry feelings will arise during the process of child rearing. All people get angry at times. Since parents are people, they get angry, too. Anger, like happiness and sadness, is a normal human emotion that we are entitled to feel and express.

We are entitled to angry feelings, but we are not entitled to angry actions. We are not entitled to lash out hurtfully at others just because we are angry. While feelings cannot be controlled, actions can. We have a choice as to how we express our anger. Either we can explode and lose control, verbally and/or physically, or we can keep our cool and express our feelings rationally and constructively. In this chapter we'll explore how we and our children can both choose the second route and learn to harness our anger and use it constructively to solve our problems.

Our uncontrolled anger can backfire on us when it comes to discipline. Some children become terribly frightened at parental anger. Just take a look in the mirror some time when you are angry, and you'll see how scary we look when we're mad. To children we may look like monsters, and they may fear that they are losing their parents. They feel rejected and abandoned. Some children are so frightened by parental outbursts that they become sneaky and deceptive, trying to avoid parental rage, while others become rageful and spiteful, deliberately disobeying their parents' wishes. Some lie just to protect themselves from experiencing parental rage. They justify it by saying, "I have to, so they won't be so angry at me." Many children model their parents' behavior and rant and rave when they are angry.

In this chapter, we will first discuss how we can manage and harness our own anger when it is triggered by our children's behavior (these anger-management techniques can be transferred to other aspects of our lives, also). Then we will discuss how we can help our children manage and harness their anger. The only way we can help our children is if we first help ourselves.

PARENTS: WHAT MAKES US ANGRY

Until I became a parent, I did not realize how many things could make me angry. Normal kids' behavior can be infuriating. Why? Sometimes their behavior makes us afraid, like when they run across the street, and we express our fear as anger. Worry and anxiety can also trigger anger, such as when our children do not come home at curfew time. Other times their fighting makes us furious because it makes us feel so helpless. We may also feel anger when we feel put-upon and overwhelmed by responsibilities. Anger often arises when we feel unsuccessful at taking care of and protecting our children.

Sometimes it is understandable when we get angry even if a child has not deliberately misbehaved. When a child spills a glass of milk all over the new carpet or accidentally breaks an irreplaceable vase, it makes sense that we might feel angry and frustrated even if it's not the child's fault. Any time that a situation puts an extra burden upon us, we may be annoyed and angry, even though the damage wasn't created intentionally.

Sometimes we get angry at children just for being children. We may expect too much, not realizing the limits of children's developmental abilities, and then we are furious when the children do not live up to our expectations. While it sure would help if he could, a two-year-old cannot be expected to get himself to bed alone. A ten-year-old cannot be expected to take care of younger children alone. A sixteen-year-old cannot always be expected to volunteer to stay home with younger siblings rather than go out with his friends. Chapter 10 provides an overview of the different stages of development and can serve as a guide in determining fair expectations. Knowing when our child is just acting like a child makes the behavior seem less annoying, and it becomes easier to keep our cool.

Sometimes our anger at our children actually has nothing whatsoever to do with what they do. Why? Because this anger may have been lurking around from our past, waiting to rear its ugly head at the slightest bit of provocation.

Baggage from Our Past
(Reminders of Our Own Sibling Rivalry)

All of us who had brothers and sisters bear scars from our sibling rivalry. When our children fight and argue with each other, memories of our fights with our siblings may be triggered. Resentments and feelings of injustice that may have been festering for years then come to the surface. Finally, after all these years, we try to set matters straight and lose control in the process.

Ted and his younger brother Patrick are playing cards. Patrick begins cheating. Ted catches him and tells him to quit it. Patrick keeps on cheating. Finally, Ted stops playing and tells Patrick he doesn't play with cheaters. Patrick runs screaming to his mother. "Mom, Ted's calling me a cheater. He won't play cards with me. I'm not a cheater. Tell him to stop." Mom jumps in, exclaiming furiously, "Ted, why are you always picking on Patrick? He's smaller than you are. Just quit it. Leave him alone."

This mother was the youngest in her family and remembers being outsmarted and picked on by her older sibling. As a parent, she now sees an opportunity to right this wrong by coming to the aid of her youngest child.

However, if the mother had been the oldest in her family, she might have angrily responded, "Just because you're the youngest, it doesn't mean you have a right to get everything you want. Don't think you can come crying and whining and get just what you want!" Having been the oldest, she might know how annoying a younger sibling's tattling can be, and thus she may angrily jump to justify her oldest's behavior.

If we were the oldest child and/or the one our parents relied on to get things done while our siblings lazily stood back, it's possible that as a child we felt put-upon and burdened by too much responsibility. Then when our children do not pitch in to help, as children are wont to do, we explode, "I can't do it all myself! Why doesn't anyone else pitch in? I'm sick and tired of having to do everything by myself!"

If one of our siblings called us a mean name that stuck, then hearing our own children do the same to each other may set us off. "Don't you ever call your brother stupid again. How can you be so mean? If you ever say that again, I'll punish you severely."

We can learn to keep our cool and not overreact in anger to our children's behavior that reminds us of infuriating situations in our own childhoods. A helpful approach is to think to yourself:

- "Does this remind me of something in my childhood? Does this remind me of how I felt as a child?"

- If the answer is yes, tell yourself, "Now is different. I am no longer a child. These children are not me and my siblings."

• Step back and look at the present situation as an outsider. Try to be as objective as you can in figuring out where the problem lies. This may not be easy to do at first, but after several tries, you will find that it works.

Baggage from Our Past
(Overidentification with Our Children)

Sometimes our children's behavior is a painful reminder of our own problems in childhood. Mr. D. was sloppy as a child. When he sees his son Nick throw his clothes around, he gets furious. He's afraid his child is picking up on his bad habits and feels to blame, but it's easier to yell at the son than to blame himself. Mrs. T. still bears scars from being left out of groups. She had a screaming battle with her daughter Sara one day because Sara chose to stay home curled up with a good book rather than go to a school dance. Mother was raging mad because she was afraid Sara would be left out of the group in the future if she did not go to the dance.

The best way to avoid overidentifying with our kids' problems that remind us of ours is to try to remember that our children are not us. They have different parents, live in a different family, and travel in a different world. Think: "My child is not me; now is different."

Baggage from Our Past
(Our Own Deprivation)

"What's he complaining about? I wish I had it that easy when I was a child." Sometimes our children's ungratefulness or complaints about their lives can be downright infuriating. We try to do what we can for them; we give them many more opportunities than we ever dreamed of having, and yet it never seems to be enough for them. We may be right, but our anger will do no good.

The best approach is to let them have their feelings, hear them out, and not get caught up arguing with them.

Baggage from Our Past
(Reminders of Our Own Rage)

Many adults who have experienced some sort of loss or trauma in childhood, and who never had a chance to process their anger, find themselves lashing out at their children for little or no reason. They know that this can hurt both them and their children. It's not that they're bad parents. It's not that they don't love their children. After years of internal suffering, they have reached a breaking point.

When Molly was eleven, her dad was killed in a car accident while he was speeding. "How could he have been so careless? Why didn't he think of us? But I can't tell anyone what I'm thinking. He's dead. It's not fair to pick on him. Everyone will think I'm mean" were thoughts that kept popping into her head.

She soon found herself getting angry at her mother as well. "I wish she were the one who died. She's so mean. She doesn't understand how I feel. I hate her. But I'd better not say anything. If I tell her, maybe she'll die, too, and then where will I be?"

Molly kept her anger locked tight inside. After all, she didn't want anyone to think she was a bad person, and she certainly didn't want to lose her mother as well.

Years passed, and Molly became a parent. She loved her children dearly but found herself getting furious at them for small offenses—talking too loudly, spilling a drink, or not saying please. Her rage seemed totally out of proportion to the situation.

What happened? When Molly was eleven, it made sense for her to be angry after her loss. Anger is a normal step in the grieving process. However, since Molly was unable to express this anger, it stayed buried inside her all through her childhood, festering below the surface, getting stronger and stronger. Finally, during adulthood, the pressure of the hidden anger inside her got so strong that it burst through the surface.

Molly's situation is all too common for many adults who have experienced the death of a loved one during childhood. Afraid that something else might happen or that they are bad people for having such feelings, many children keep pushing the rage down inside them. Then one day, as adults, they can push no more, and the rage explodes on an innocent target, often their children.

The same happens for adults who were abused or mistreated as children. When they were children, they had every right to be angry. It's not fair or right when children are hurt either intentionally or accidentally. However, abused or neglected children cannot direct anger onto the person who is mistreating them lest it trigger even worse mistreatment. So they must keep it stuffed inside. Years later, as adults, they may find their rage bursting out, often on their own children.

If you feel that anger you have been stuffing inside you since childhood may now be coming to the surface, try following the steps for harnessing your anger on pages 91–95. While you are taking these steps, try to stay focused on the events at hand. If you find your anger oozing out everywhere anyway, seek professional help in overcoming this problem.

What happened to you in your childhood was indeed unfair. As a child you had every right to be angry. But it is also unfair for you to take out this anger on your own children. Working through your hidden anger with a professional will be one of the greatest gifts you will ever give both yourself and your children. You all deserve it. Please see Chapter 12 for guidance in seeking professional help.

Bringing up children sure is a challenge for parents. All of us get angry at our children at times. As parents, we must try to take a step back, look at what makes us angry, decide how we can get to the primary feeling beneath the rage, and then express it constructively. If the anger has hidden sources in our own past, we can work on identifying and rooting out these hidden sources.

HOW WE CAN HARNESS OUR ANGER

Anger in and of itself isn't bad. When expressed destructively by verbal or physical lashing out at others, anger serves no useful purpose. However, when expressed constructively and nonhurtfully, anger can be a terrific motivator for effecting change. Just think how the civil rights movement channeled anger over segregation into a major transformation of our society. Let's look at how we can harness anger in a way that will be worthwhile for our well-being and the well-being of our children and in a way that can help us produce positive results.

Harnessing our *own* anger is the first step. Then we can teach our children how to do the same. If Dad throws a fit every time he is asked to help someone around the house, if Mom starts screaming every time the children fight, if we get raging mad at their outbursts, then our children will learn to have fits and scream when they are angry. Just as with the rest of our behavior, our children will copy how we express our anger. Usually, the way we parents handle anger is the same way our children handle their anger. Let's look at a successful approach for harnessing anger.

Step One: Noticing Our Body's Message

"I was burning mad." "I was so angry my heart was beating a mile a minute." "I was so angry I felt like crying." "Every time I get angry, I grind my teeth." Our bodies have extraordinary ways of letting us know when we are angry and about to "lose it"— tensed muscles, crying, laughing, burning, heart palpitating twitching, teeth grinding, stone silence, and shaking are all wa' our bodies signal our anger.

Try to figure out your body's way of expressing anger, and you may be able to identify that angry feeling before it overtakes you. If you can tune in to your body's signals that you are angry, you can catch yourself before you say or do something you will later regret. The next time you get angry, try to notice changes you feel in your body—temperature, muscles, body movements. Are you shaky, hot, cold, or stiff? Are you grinding your teeth or clenching your fists? Is your heart beating fast or your head hurting? Do you feel like crying? Is there anything else you notice happening to your body when you are angry?

By listening to our body's message, we can become aware of our rising anger and harness it before it reaches a crescendo and gets out of control.

Step Two: Collecting Ourselves

Once we hear our body signaling that we are about to lose our temper, we can try to collect ourselves. We can take action to stop ourselves from going over the edge and doing something we may later regret. We don't have to be angry to teach discipline. Only when we are calm will we be able to be clear about what we want and to do what is fair.

Different approaches to collecting oneself will work for different people. Here are some suggestions you might like to try. Only you can figure out what activity works best for you. You may find something that you like even better than any of these suggestions:

- If your children are old enough to be left alone or if there is another adult with your children, go somewhere else until you can collect yourself. Tell your children what you are doing. Take a walk or go to another room. Try to stay away no longer than five or ten minutes. When you come back, then you can talk.

- Listen to music—whatever music is calming and soothing to you.

- Take a few deep breaths. Deep breathing exercises might be helpful.

- Count backward from ten to one.

- Try to do something with your hands to keep them busy—bake a cake, wash a counter, draw, write down what you are feeling, or even just scribble.

- To help yourself not say anything you'll be sorry for later, chew gum, sing, even put your hand up to your mouth.

- Get some physical exercise.

Step Three: Talking

Talking about anger can only be done when we are relatively calm. If your anger takes hold of you and you feel blinded by rage, be sure you have followed the first two steps before you even begin to talk about the problem.

Give voice to your anger rather than letting it fester inside you. People who bottle up their anger often take it out on those around them. Many are just downright negative people. Try to put your feelings into words. But remember to do so constructively. An "I message" can be very effective (see pages 68–71).

Let them know how you feel.

Start with the words "I feel." Hearing that you have feelings usually arouses empathy and consideration. Children are more likely to listen if you focus on your own emotions rather than on criticizing their behavior and blaming them for your emotions. Hearing "You drive me crazy" or "You make me mad" usually arouses defensiveness and hostility and can backfire on you.

Zero in on the real feelings that lie below your anger. Anger is a catch-all expression used for all kinds of feelings. Try to be more specific about how you feel. For example: "I feel *worried* when I don't know where you are and it's past your curfew"; "I feel *frustrated* when I spend hours cleaning, and five minutes later the house is a mess again"; "I feel *put-upon* when I've worked all day and then I have to do all the laundry myself even though I'm tired"; "I feel *uncomfortable* when there's bickering and company is at the house"; "I feel *overwhelmed* when I have to face the dishes after cooking supper"; I feel *embarrassed* when people think I haven't taught you manners"; "I feel *afraid* when you disappear from my sight in the store"; "I feel *disappointed* when my trust is violated." There are many other feelings you may find at the base of your anger. Try to get in touch with these primary feelings and put them into words.

Let them know when you feel this way.

Describe the *situation*, not the person, that triggered the negative feelings. "I feel put-upon when there are clothes all over the floor." "I feel frustrated when as soon as I finish cleaning up, there is another mess." Avoid using the word *you* in an accusatory fashion such as "I feel put-upon when *you* are such a slob" or "I feel frustrated because *you* are so undependable." The accusatory *you* puts the child on the defensive.

Let them know why you feel this way.

Explain why the situation makes you have negative feelings. This sells your message. "I am annoyed when there are clothes all over the floor because someone might trip on them." "I feel overwhelmed when there are dishes in the sink because then I have to put them all away and I am tired." The *because* shows the child that you have a legitimate reason for your feelings. Perhaps just making a statement will be sufficient to resolve the issue. "I feel embarrassed when there are jackets on the furniture and company comes." Hearing this, the children may clean up their jackets immediately.

Other times, after you have made this statement, the next step is to set a consequence for the behavior. "I am disappointed that you rode your bike to town when you were told not to. I am worried that you could get hurt. As a consequence, you cannot ride your bike for the rest of the week."

Other times it may mean that you can then try to solve the problem together. "I feel put-upon when I come home from work and I have to still clean and cook. Let's figure out what we can do about this."

We have a right to our feelings, including anger, but we do not have the right to lash out at our children physically, verbally, or emotionally. By using the general "I message" formula ("I feel———when———because———") we can express what we feel without attacking our children and putting them on the defensive. Often children do not stop to think that we are also human beings with feelings. This happens not out of maliciousness but because of the self-centeredness that is part of a child's nature. This also happens because we often tend to tiptoe around our children, hide our feelings, and not be honest and straightforward in expressing our feelings to our children. We may be afraid of how they might react.

CHILDREN: WHAT MAKES THEM ANGRY

When they can't go out to play ball, when they can't borrow the car, when they lose a privilege because they have misbehaved, we can expect that our children will be angry. Often children get angry when disciplined. They can't have what they want, they don't like it, they're disappointed, and that makes them angry.

When a child is racing with another child, falls down, and then blames the other runner for running too fast; when a child who is asked to help out is angry at the imposition on him; when a child misbehaves and is angry at the person for catching him; the anger is unjustified. They mess up and try to place the blame for their mistake on others. They project their frustration or embarrassment onto someone else in the form of anger.

Accept children's right to their own feelings even if you don't agree with them. Let them get angry, but you keep your cool. Don't make it contagious.

Power Struggles

One surefire way to get both us and our children really riled up at the same time is to get into a power struggle with them. "You're supposed to——," "No, I won't," "Do it right now," "No, I'm not doing it," "Yes, you are," "You can't make me," "Oh, I can't? You'll see!" We feel that we need to be in control, yet at the same time our children are struggling to assert themselves and establish their own identities and status. Here are some ways to avoid raging power struggles.

- Give them choices that we can accept rather than decreeing that they *have to* do something. By having a choice, they feel they have some control over the situation. Instead of telling them they have to wear their socks, ask them, "Would you like to wear the red socks or the blue socks?" Instead of telling them they have to help clean up the kitchen, give them a choice of chores—washing or drying the dishes, sweeping the floor, or clearing the table.

- Choose your battles. If a child wants to wear a hat to bed, what harm does it do? If a child wants to wear striped shirt and checkered pants, what harm does it do? Some parents fear that if they give in on small things like the hat or the outfit, then they will lose their authority and control. Children don't operate that way. If we let children have their say in matters that really are not critical, then they will be more likely, not less likely, to listen to us when the critical matters arise.

• If you do get into a power struggle, as happens to most of us at one time or another, don't try to outshout them. Try to stay calm, keep your voice low, and keep your dignity. Try to find an escape for both of you, even using humor if you can. Saving face is very important to children.

Harnessing Children's Anger

The same approach you use for harnessing your own anger will work with your children, too. Some children learn how to manage their anger just by watching us. Others need to be directly taught anger management.

Give them an opportunity to talk and you listen. Help them express their feelings just as you do: I feel———when——— because———. Listen very carefully. Draw out their feelings. As we listen to them express anger, if they go on the attack and divert blame and responsibility away from themselves, we can gently guide our children to accept personal responsibility and reach down to the primary feeling below the anger. "Yes, you would rather read than take out the trash. It's frustrating to have to stop in the middle of a good part."

The key for the adult is to be a good listener. Listening to them does not mean that you have to agree with them. Don't take their anger personally or get frightened or wounded by their anger. Try to restate what you think they are feeling to see if you are under-standing them correctly: "So, it sounds like you're really frustrated because———." If you have not understood them, they will set you straight. Try not to argue with their reasoning: "You don't have a right to feel that way because———." Try not to argue with them about how they feel: "C'mon. You don't really feel that way." Just try to be accepting of their feelings.

Sometimes just giving voice to their anger is sufficient. Other times it may be necessary to help them use the problem-solving steps (chapter 8) to try to work through a solution to their problem.

If your children get extremely agitated when angry, then it may be helpful to teach them how to collect themselves first before they talk. This teaching should be saved for a calm time, not in the heat of anger.

First, teach them how to identify their body's anger signals: "You're grinding your teeth. I guess you must be pretty angry." "You're clenching your fists. Are you angry?" If you figure out your children's particular characteristics when they are angry, you can point out these characteristics to them. Soon they will be able to recognize on their own when they are about to "lose it."

Then, teach them how to collect themselves. Show them techniques for cooling down so that they will not do something they will later regret. Some helpful ways for children to collect themselves are:

+ Take time-out. They may need to be off by themselves for a few minutes to calm themselves down. This is not the same as sending children to time-out as punishment. This kind of time-out is designed to give children an opportunity to collect their thoughts, take a break from a heated situation, and calm themselves down. It should not be used as a punishment for anger, rather as an aid in anger management.

+ Go to another room and scream. It sometimes helps just to release tension.

+ Draw, scribble, or write. Sometimes writing a letter to the person they are angry at helps.

+ Play with clay. Twisting and turning something concrete like clay can release negative energy.

- Build or make something. Sometimes just hammering helps children (if you consider it safe for them to have a hammer).

- Listen to music. Let them choose the music; what is calming to us may drive them crazy and vice versa.

- Exercise. Physically letting out some of that energy can help.

- Hug a stuffed animal.

Summary

Anger in and of itself is not bad. When uncontrolled, it can do great harm. But when harnessed and expressed constructively, it can have positive outcomes. Just as with all other matters of behavior, our children learn from what we do, not what we say. We as parents must first learn to harness our own anger; then we can teach our children to harness theirs.

SUMMARY OF MAIN POINTS

- As people and parents, we have a right to be angry at times.

- People cannot control their feelings, including anger, but they can control their actions.

- Parents never have the right to take out their anger hurtfully on their children.

- Parents can learn how to harness their anger, express it constructively, and effect positive changes.

- Parents can teach their children how to harness their anger, express it constructively, and effect positive changes.

CHAPTER SEVEN

What to Do After Children Misbehave

Sometimes we can prevent misbehavior from happening. Setting fair, meaningful limits is certainly a major step in this direction. Another step is to eliminate temptations—by removing breakable objects from the reach of a young child, covering up the electrical outlets, not teaching a child to drive at age thirteen and then leaving car keys around, or not leaving the house when teens are having a party and might be tempted to drink. Yet another way to prevent misbehavior is to distract or divert children. This works very well with young children. When a child is writing on a book, give her paper instead; when a child takes his sister's toy, interest him in a different toy; when a child is acting up in the car, get her to count license plates or listen to a story tape.

Other times, though, we have to do something *after* our children misbehave. No matter how well we set down limits or how well we remove temptations, no matter how wonderful our kids are and how sensitive we are as parents, our children will still misbehave and we will have to do something about it. Our children are new at the game of life; they are bound to make mistakes. Think back to a time when you were first learning something new, perhaps a new sport. Didn't you make mistakes as you practiced?

When a child misbehaves, we usually need to respond to the misbehavior. Fortunately, there are times when we don't have to do too much. These times call for low-key discipline. At other times, we have to react more strongly, using major discipline approaches.

LOW-KEY DISCIPLINE

Although our children's misbehavior usually calls for some sort of response from us, in most situations we fortunately do not have to do too much. We can do something minor to nip the problem in the bud. Signaling, reminding, warning, ignoring, praising, and just stopping and doing nothing will work. We can call these tools for redirecting the inappropriate behavior before it becomes a major discipline problem *low-key discipline.*

Signaling

Nonverbal.

"The look" can sometimes work miracles with our children. One good long, hard stare from us and they settle right down. Eyes can speak.

Signaling with our hands can also be an effective discipline tool. Raising a finger to our lips when we want them to be quiet in a public place or pointing to clothes left on the floor can get our message across clearly but silently.

Verbal.

"I messages" (see pages 68–71) can be a highly effective tool for getting our children to listen to us when we see a problem we want to change. Rather than lashing out at them, we describe the situation calmly and clearly, making it likely that our children will do what they are supposed to do on their own without being told.

Reminding

Don't Litter signs remind us of a rule we should already know. Every once in a while we all need reminders—especially children. Sometimes children honestly forget rules or get so carried away that they lose sight of them. Just reminding the child about a rule may be enough to stop the misbehavior. "Remember, we throw balls outside, not inside," or "Remember, your curfew is midnight."

Warning

Perhaps you can think back to how appreciative you were when a police officer gave you a warning rather than a ticket. You probably watched your speed after that. Sometimes a warning is just enough to get us back on track. Warning a child what will happen if he does the same thing again may work at times: "The next time you are sassy to me when talking to your friends on the phone, I will take away your phone privileges," or "The next time you throw the ball in the house, I will take it away." Warnings only work if they are given once or twice. If we warn over and over again about the same thing, then our children will know that we don't really mean what we are saying. If a child still misbehaves after being warned, then we need to follow through with the consequences we promised.

Ignoring

Ignoring a minor problem, for example, "not noticing" when children get into a little squabble, may be the best approach for us at times. Why not save our energy for bigger problems? But ignoring small infractions is not the same as ignoring our children when they are seeking attention. If a child is deliberately misbehaving to attract our attention, ignoring this misbehavior will probably result only in its escalation. After all, when a child is feeling needy, isn't negative attention better than no attention at all? The bottom line: ignoring small, perhaps unintentional mistakes is sometimes an effective low-key discipline strategy, but ignoring deliberate, attention-getting misbehavior can backfire.

Praising

It is human nature that when we are encouraged about something we are doing, we will be more likely to do it again. Praising a child when he does something right even though at other times he may do it wrong may inspire him to do the right thing more often: "You cleaned up your room very well today," or "Your table manners were great at breakfast." Place the emphasis on the positive, not the negative.

Noticing slight positive changes in behavior can encourage a child to continue in that direction. However, sometimes praise can be discouraging or counterproductive and can even lead children to further misbehavior. For example, praising a child at the expense of another—"You cleaned up much faster than your brother"—may result in a squabble between siblings. Please see chapter 4 for a detailed discussion of appropriate and inappropriate uses of praise.

Doing Nothing

Sometimes if we just stop dead in our tracks, saying and doing nothing, the shock may remind our children to shape up. For example, my husband and I found that an effective tool to stop our children from bickering in the car when chauffeuring them around to activities was to find a safe spot, pull the car over, and just sit there until the bickering stopped.

MAJOR DISCIPLINE

Sometimes low-key discipline does not work, and we need a stronger, more direct approach that will teach children not to misbehave again. This involves trying to figure out why the child misbehaved and making changes that will prevent the misbehavior from being repeated. These changes may include setting consequences if the misbehavior was intentional.

Why Kids Misbehave

Don't take misbehavior personally. While it may not seem that way upon first glance, kids *usually* misbehave to meet their own needs, not to take revenge on us. Try to eliminate all other possibilities before interpreting poor behavior as a personal affront.

Sometimes children misbehave because they are not physically ready for what they are doing. A two-year-old may keep spilling her milk because she cannot handle the cup. A five-year-old may break thin crayons because it is difficult for him to color gently. Other times, children misbehave because they are not mentally ready. A three-year-old may run into the street because he cannot understand the dangers involved. A teenager may drive fast because he thinks he'll live forever. If physical or mental immaturity is causing the misbehavior, then we must take control to assure that our child is not injured. (Chapter 10 discusses in detail what's fair to expect of children at each age.)

Normal curiosity leads to misbehavior at times. The children's book character Curious George is an excellent example of misbehavior caused by curiosity. A two-year-old may keep spilling milk trying to figure out the properties of liquid. A ten-year-old may ruin a watch trying to understand how it works. If curiosity leads to misbehavior, a consequence that helps the child fix up the damage and an explanation of what she did wrong may be the best approach.

Many times, children misbehave to meet their own needs—to make themselves feel important, to be the one in charge, to feel accepted, to have a good time, to get out their anger, or to get people to notice them. A nine-year-old may go where he's told not to. A teen may stay out beyond his curfew. Kids fight and curse. These are the most challenging discipline problems. Having them experience a consequence for their misbehavior and figure out what they can do to prevent it from happening again is an approach that works.

It is important that we figure out how we can help the child not make the same mistake again. This means first looking at the reasons *why* the child misbehaved in that situation and then trying to do something about the *why*. Sometimes just separating the hitter for a while is not enough to get him to stop hitting. If we look at *why* he hits, we may find out that it is because he does not know what else to do when he is angry. If this is the case, preventing future misconduct means teaching him how to put his feelings into words instead of actions.

The following chart summarizes some of the *whys* of misbehavior and what we can do about them.

THE WHYS OF MISBEHAVIOR AND
WHAT WE CAN DO ABOUT THEM

Why Might This Child Be Misbehaving?	What Can I Do About It?
Inexperience or ignorance	• State expectations clearly and directly. • Demonstrate and practice appropriate behavior.
Physical immaturity	• Adjust expectations.
Emotional immaturity	• Adjust expectations. • Teach appropriate behavior.
Curiosity	• Allow free time to explore. • Restrict access to breakables. • Require repairing damage.
Need for belonging	• Give child responsibilities. • Provide opportunities for involvement with others.
Need for recognition	• Give child responsibility, recognition, and opportunities to shine.
Need for power or control	• Provide choices and opportunities for decision making. • Engage child in problem solving. • Give child responsibility.
Anger release	• Allow child to express feelings. • Practice anger harnessing with child.

Why Might This Child Be Misbehaving?	What Can I Do About It?
Enjoyment, adventure, and fun	• *Make child aware of problem.* • *Provide a consequence for the behavior.* • *Engage in problem solving.*
Fear	• *Listen and engage in problem solving.*
Feelings of ineptness	• *Listen.* • *Give child responsibility.* • *Engage in problem solving.*
Stress	• *Eliminate stressors.* • *Listen to child.* • *Practice stress reduction exercises.*

Consequences for Misbehavior

In some cases, it is important for children to assume responsibility and to make amends for their inappropriate behavior. That's where consequences come in. Consequences teach children that their actions have effects. Four categories of consequences for teaching responsibility are restoration or restitution, composure, restriction, and reflection.

Restoration or restitution.

When a person messes up, or breaks or loses someone else's property, whether it's intentional or not, the responsible, right thing to do is either fix or restore the item to its original state, if possible, or make restitution. Therefore, the appropriate consequence for the child who spills milk would be to have the child help clean up the milk. If one sister borrows another's shirt and dirties it, she should clean the shirt before returning it. If a teen dents the car, he should earn money to pay for the damage.

Composure.

Sometimes, when children get out of control, they need time and space to restore themselves, to collect themselves so that they can function civilly with others. That's where time-out as a consequence comes in. When our child "loses it," we can matter-of-factly and respectfully guide our child to a time-out area where he or she can read, write, draw, listen to music, rock on a rocking chair, hug a stuffed animal—whatever will help the child to restore his or her composure and rejoin the rest of the family. This form of time-out is totally different from the time-out that is a punishment used as a main discipline tool. The time-out we are referring to should not be viewed as a punishment but rather as an opportunity for the child to reestablish equilibrium.

Restriction.

Sometimes, when children abuse privileges, an appropriate consequence is to restrict that privilege temporarily. If a child misuses the computer and logs on to forbidden sites, then restricting the child from using the computer makes sense. If a child cheats while playing cards, excluding him from the next one or two card games might discourage future cheating. If a young child runs toward the street, bringing him/her inside immediately should get the message across.

Reflection.

Often, the most effective tool for preventing the repetition of misbehavior is having children reflect about the problem and figure out how they can prevent themselves from getting into the same situation again. In chapter 8, we will discuss how problem solving can be used as a tool for this reflection.

Choosing a Consequence

Here are some questions I have found helpful to ask when choosing a consequence:

- ◆ Does it make sense? Does it logically follow from what the child did? Is it related to the misbehavior?

- ◆ Does it make the child accountable for his or her actions? Is the child responsible for correcting any damage or harm caused by the misbehavior? Is it a learning situation?

- ◆ Above all, does it keep the child's and my dignity intact?

How Consequences Differ from Punishments

Some people might call this aspect of discipline punishment, but punishment differs from consequences in several ways. Punishment implies getting back at children. Often, the intent of punishment is to make children so uncomfortable that they will be afraid to misbehave. The intent of consequences, though, is to teach them *why* they should not make the same mistake again. While punishments are often not even connected to what the child did wrong, consequences must be. Punishment places the responsibility for correction in the hands of the parents. Consequences place the responsibility for correction in the hands of the child by requiring that she correct the damage or harm caused by her misbehavior whenever possible. Consequences are ever mindful of the dignity of both children and parents. Punishment often sacrifices dignity to get the point across.

Let's look at some examples:

Does it make sense?

Consequences flow logically from what the child did. They should be related to the misbehavior and make sense. Punishments are often not even connected to what the child did wrong.

Example: Two children are fighting.

Consequence: After cooling down, both children are required to sit down, discuss their problem, and work out a solution together.

Punishment: Both children are spanked.

Does it make the child accountable?

Consequences make the children accountable for their behavior. They place the responsibility for correction in the hands of children by requiring that they correct the damage or harm caused by the misbehavior whenever possible or by requiring that children figure out alternative, acceptable behaviors for themselves. Punishments place the responsibility for correction in the hands of the parent.

Example: A child writes on the wall.

Consequence: The child must clean the wall.

Punishment: The child is sent to time-out to think about what he did (while the parent fumes and cleans the wall).

Is everyone's dignity intact?

Consequences keep our children's and our dignity intact. Punishments are often humiliating.

Example: A child takes his sibling's crayons.

Consequence: Private discussion with the child about the ramifications of taking something without asking and helping the child plan for how to avoid this in the future.

Punishment: Yell at the child, call him a thief.

The bottom line is that appropriate consequences help our children become more responsible. Using punishments to get back at children for misbehaving can be counterproductive.

SUMMARY OF MAIN POINTS

◆ Some misbehavior can be prevented, but some cannot.

◆ There are times when reminding, warning, ignoring, praising or doing nothing will stop misbehavior.

◆ There are times when misbehavior is due to immaturity. The parents must assume responsibility for better supervision and guidance.

◆ There are other times when a strong, direct approach to misbehavior is needed.

◆ Often children must experience consequences for their misbehavior.

◆ Consequences for misbehavior teach children that their actions have effects.

◆ Consequences are not the same as punishments.

CHAPTER EIGHT

Problem Solving: A Tool for Parents and Children

What makes discipline so challenging is that misbehavior is such a complicated issue. Children misbehave for all sorts of reasons and in all sorts of ways. It sure would be convenient to find one answer that would work all the time, but a one-size-fits-all solution simply does not exist. Fortunately, however, there is a skill we can learn that will help us find the answers: problem solving. Problem solving can be a terrific vehicle for determining our course of action when regarding discipline issues. We can use the problem-solving process to help us figure out what causes the misbehavior, how we can prevent future problems, and how we can select appropriate consequences. In addition, we can guide our children to use the problem-solving process themselves to figure out how to replace inappropriate behavior with appropriate behavior and how to resolve their conflicts with each other.

Problem solving works splendidly when figuring out how to discipline children. As an added advantage, once you learn this skill, you'll find it applicable in other aspects of your life. Problem solving is an incredible tool because it can be used in so many different ways. Businesspeople use it to design new products, mediators use it for conflict resolution, and mathematicians use it to solve math problems. Research has shown that problem solving increases student achievement in school. As you become experienced in problem solving, you can also teach these techniques to your children. They will be able to use problem solving in many aspects of their own lives, from improving their schoolwork to improving their behavior.

Keep in mind that at first this process may be awkward and time-consuming for us and for our children. But, with practice, the thought patterns will soon become automatic.

There are seven basic steps to the problem-solving process. After an explanation of each of the problem-solving steps, we will look at how they apply to specific discipline problems.

1. State the problem.

Before you can figure out a solution, you have to know what the problem is. Try to summarize problems in one or two sentences.

2. Brainstorm ideas.

Try to come up with as many ideas for solving the problem as possible, and write them down. Don't worry about whether the ideas are good or not; just try to find lots of them. One idea leads to another. A bad idea may lead to a good idea. Quantity, not quality, is what you should aim for at this stage.

3. Evaluate the ideas.

Carefully look at each idea you came up with in step #2. Keep in mind both the people involved and the situation. Do you think it will work? If so, why? If not, why? Is it acceptable to everyone involved (in our case both the parents and the children)? Some ideas may be acceptable to some people and not to others.

4. Select an idea.

The key is to find an idea that is acceptable to all parties concerned and which you think will work best to solve the problem stated in #1. (More information on this step will be supplied when we discuss specific examples.)

5. Try out the idea.

Implement the solution you chose in the previous step.

6. Evaluate effectiveness.

See if the solution you chose is working. Did it solve the problem you described in step #1?

7. Decide.

If your answer to step #6 is yes and the solution solves the problem, then you are finished. Mission accomplished. If, however, your answer is no, do not get discouraged. Either return to step #4 and choose another solution, return to step #2 to design more solutions, or return to step #1 to be sure you put your finger on the real problem. Be sure not to give up if the problem remains. You will be able to solve it if you don't give up.

PROBLEM SOLVING FOR
DISCIPLINE PURPOSES

Let's look at some real-life examples that show how problem solving can help us figure out what to do when children misbehave. We'll slowly go through each of the problem-solving steps to show you how you can do it. With practice, these steps will become automatic and won't take so much time.

Example: Three-year-old Amy has been told repeatedly not to play with her milk. She was playing with her milk and spilled it on the floor.

I. Problem Solving: Figuring Out the Cause

We only need to use the first four problem-solving steps to identify the source of the problem, or why it happened.

1. State the problem.
Why did Amy spill her milk?

2. Brainstorm ideas.
Try to think of as many ideas as you can for why Amy spilled the milk. Remember to first look at physical or mental immaturity.

- "Her cup was too big and she could not handle it."
- "She was not hungry."
- "She hates milk."
- "She did it just because she wanted to disobey me."

3. Evaluate the ideas.

* *Cup too big:*

"Since she easily drinks juice out of this cup, I know she can handle it."

* *Not hungry:*

"She was probably not too full because she ate everything else after she spilled her milk."

* *Hates milk:*

"I'm not sure whether she hates milk. She doesn't say so, but she does not look very happy when I put it on her high chair."

* *Testing me:*

"She may be testing me to see what I will do when she disobeys, in which case having her clean up the mess should get her to stop."

4. Select an idea.

"I think the problem is that Amy is spilling her milk because she does not like milk." (In this case, we are assuming this is the problem. In other cases, the problem may differ.)

II. Problem Solving: Preventing Future Problems

Now it's time to change the environment to prevent this problem from happening again.

1. State the problem.

"How can I get Amy to drink her milk and not spill it, even though she does not like it?"

2. Brainstorm ideas.

* "I could give her chocolate milk."

+ "I could give her something else to replace the milk she needs for growing, like yogurt and cheese."
+ "I just won't give her milk."

3. Evaluate the ideas.

+ *Give her chocolate milk:*
"Chocolate milk is too sweet and not so healthy."
+ *Give her yogurt and cheese:*
"She does like other dairy products like yogurt and cheese."
+ *Not give her milk:*
"I can't just not give her milk, because she needs it for her health."

4. Select an idea.

"Therefore, I'll stop giving her milk to drink and instead give her cheese and yogurt."

5. Try out the idea.

Mother gives Amy yogurt and cheese instead of milk.

6. Evaluate effectiveness.

She loves the yogurt and doesn't have any milk to spill.

7. Decide.

Amy isn't spilling her milk anymore, so the problem is solved.

If instead you found that Amy was still spilling her drink, you could go back to determining the reasons (see page 115) and look at the other possible explanations for her spilling. For example, if you decided instead that maybe the cup was too big, you could brainstorm such relevant solutions as using a smaller cup or using a cup with a lid.

III. Problem Solving: Selecting Appropriate Consequences

You may also feel that a consequence would be appropriate in this situation since Amy deliberately spilled her milk.

1. State the problem.

The problem is that Amy played with her milk when she was not supposed to and now there's milk all over the floor. How can I provide a consequence for this behavior?

2. Brainstorm ideas.

Here is the list of consequences her mother thought up to solve the problem:

- "I won't refill her cup."
- "I will send her to time-out."
- "I'll have her clean up the milk."
- "I'll spank her."
- "I'll yell at her."

3. Evaluate the ideas.

The guidelines mentioned previously are helpful for selecting a consequence: Does it make sense? Does it make the child accountable? Does it preserve our dignity? Amy's mother needs to answer these questions for each of the consequences she thought up in step #2:

- "*I won't refill her cup.* It makes some sense because it might help her learn not to play with her milk again. But it doesn't make complete sense not to give her more milk because she needs milk to grow. It might prevent repetition, although the milk would still have to be cleaned up this time and I'd probably have to do it."

• *"I will send her to time-out.* It makes sense to send her away from the table if she can't behave properly, but she's so young she may not understand the connection between spilled milk and isolation. Time-out might not prevent repetition and certainly doesn't make her responsible for cleaning up the milk. She needs milk to grow, so this would not be an appropriate solution."

• *"I'll have her clean up the milk.* It makes sense that if you spill something you clean it up. If she has the responsibility of cleaning it up, she'll probably be more careful next time, so it would prevent repetition."

• *"I'll spank her.* Spanking and spilling milk aren't connected. It doesn't make sense, but it might make her afraid ever to play with her milk, preventing her from doing it again. The milk would still have to be cleaned up, and I'd probably have to do it."

• *"I'll yell at her* I feel like yelling because I'm so angry, but it doesn't make sense. It will just scare her and might make her either afraid to play with her milk or so nervous that she spills the milk again. It's not clear whether yelling will prevent this from happening again, and I'd still have to clean up the milk."

Let's make a chart of our three questions for evaluating our ideas and look at how each idea fits in.

WHAT TO DO AFTER YOUR CHILD MISBEHAVES

Consequence	Make Sense?	Make Accountable?	Preserve Dignity?
No milk	?	no	yes
Time-out	yes	no	yes
Child clean up	yes	yes	yes
Spank	no	no	no
Yell	no	no	no

4. Select an idea.

Looking at the chart, we see that cleaning up the milk is the only consequence where the answer to all three questions is *yes*. Amy's mom chose to have Amy clean up the milk.

5. Try out the idea.

Mother handed Amy a cloth and told her, "The milk is spilled; please clean it up," and guided her in doing it correctly. (Young children might need help in fixing up the damage they have caused. Use your own judgment.)

The way you tell the child the consequence influences how well your child will obey you. Try to stay calm and matter-of-fact. "The milk is spilled; please clean it up," rather than "Clean that up right this minute!" If your tone is demanding and threatening, your child might become defensive or rebellious and refuse to do it.

6. Evaluate effectiveness.
   Amy cleaned up the milk.

7. Decide.
   The consequence was carried out.

> **Example: Two-year-old Tommy pulls his baby brother's hair until the baby cries.**

I. Problem Solving: Figuring Out the Cause

1. State the problem.
   "Why is Tommy pulling his baby brother's hair?"

2. Brainstorm ideas.
   * "Tommy is jealous for my attention."
   * "He is just curious about the baby."
   * "He does not realize that he is hurting the baby."

3. Evaluate the ideas.
   * *Jealous:*
   "Tommy may be jealous. I have been busy with the baby and have had little time to spend alone with Tommy."
   * *Curious:*
   "Since he's never been around babies before, he may be curious."
   * *Not realize hurt:*
   "Tommy probably does know it hurts. After all, he knows it hurts him when another child pulls his hair."

4. Select an idea.

In this case, the first two reasons make sense, and so preventing Tommy from pulling the baby's hair could involve solutions to both of these reasons. (When problem solving, you can have more than one reason for a problem. At these times it's usually best to try out the solutions for the different reasons at the same time.)

II. Problem Solving: Preventing Future Problems

1. State the problem.

"How can I help Tommy not be so jealous of the baby, and how can I satisfy his curiosity so he won't pull the baby's hair?"

2. Brainstorm ideas.

- "I can take Tommy out for the day."
- "I can spend more time with Tommy when the baby is asleep."
- "I can read to Tommy while nursing the baby."
- "I'll show him how to touch the baby gently."
- "I'll be sure he's not alone with the baby."
- "I'll just tell him to leave the baby alone."

3. Evaluate the ideas.

- *Out for the day:*

"Since I'm nursing, I can't take Tommy out for the day."

- *Play when baby sleeps:*

"I'll have time to play with him when the baby is asleep."

- *Read when nursing:*

"I can also read to him while I'm feeding the baby."

- *Show how to touch:*

"He may not know how to touch the baby, so I'll show him."

♦ *Not leave alone:*
"Until the baby is a little older, I won't leave them alone."
♦ *Tell no:*
"Just telling Tommy to leave the baby alone won't work because I don't think he'll listen."

4. Select an idea.

"Therefore, I'll try to spend more time with Tommy when the baby is asleep and read to him when I am nursing the baby. I'll also show him how to touch the baby gently, but, just to be sure, I won't leave him alone in the room with the baby."

5. Try out the idea.

Tommy's mother spends more time with him when the baby's asleep and reads to him when she can, including when she's nursing the baby. She makes sure not to leave Tommy alone with the baby, but she also shows him how to touch the baby.

6. Evaluate effectiveness.

Tommy no longer pulls the baby's hair.

7. Decide.

The problem is solved.

III. Problem Solving: Selecting Appropriate Consequences

1. State the problem.

"What consequence will follow when Tommy pulls the baby's hair?"

2. Brainstorm ideas.
    * "I could spank Tommy."
    * "I could yell at him."
    * "I could tell him, 'No, hair-pulling hurts.' "
    * "I could say, 'No, that hurts' and take him away from the baby."
    * "I could pull Tommy's hair to show him what it feels like."

3. Evaluate the ideas.
    * *Spank* : "If I hurt him, how can I expect him not to hurt someone else?"
    * *Yell:* "Yelling at a two-year-old doesn't make much sense. He probably won't understand what I'm so hysterical about. Since he won't understand, it won't prevent him from doing it again. It also focuses my attention on him instead of on the baby, and he may like that."
    * *Tell no:* "Hair-pulling does hurt, so it makes sense to tell him that. Maybe if he knows it hurts, he won't do it again, but it's still risky leaving him near the baby."
    * *Tell no and take away:* "Hair-pulling does hurt, so it makes sense to tell him that. If I take him away, he can't hurt the baby, and maybe he'll figure out not to do it again."
    * *Pull hair:* "That's just doing what he did wrong."

Let's look at how these solutions fit into our chart.

WHAT TO DO AFTER YOUR CHILD MISBEHAVES

Consequence	Make Sense?	Make Accountable?	Preserve Dignity?
Spank	no	no	no
Yell	no	no	no
Say no	yes	no	yes
Say no, remove	yes	yes	yes
Pull hair	no	no	no

4. Select an idea.

We cannot expect a two-year-old to be responsible for his own behavior. Telling him, "No, hair pulling hurts," and taking him away for a few minutes seems to best meet the criteria for good consequences. Explaining why not to do something is very important, even for a two-year-old, who may not speak well. Even very young children need to know reasons.

5. Try out the idea.

The next time Tommy pulled the baby's hair, his mother told him, "No, hair pulling hurts," and took him out of the room.

6. Evaluate effectiveness.

Tommy couldn't pull the baby's hair because he was not near the baby.

7. Decide.

This solves the problem for right now, but she'll have to figure out how to prevent it from happening another time.

Example: Two-year-old Jenna was playing in the yard. She was told to stay only in the yard. Suddenly her cat ran by, and she chased it into the street.

I. Problem Solving: Figuring Out the Cause

1. State the problem.

Why did Jenna run out into the street?

2. Brainstorm ideas.

- She doesn't know any better.
- She doesn't listen and obey.

3. Evaluate the ideas.

- *Not know any better:*

Jenna is only two years old. Children this age do not understand that they can be hurt.

- *Doesn't listen and obey:*

Children this age can be easily distracted and often do not remember or understand rules.

4. Select an idea.

Jenna is too young to understand about running into the street.

II. Problem Solving: Selecting Appropriate Consequences

1. State the problem.

"What would be an appropriate consequence when Jenna runs into the street?"

2. Brainstorm ideas.

- "I could spank her."
- "I could yell at her and tell her never to do that again."
- "I could say, 'No, you can get hurt' and take her firmly by the hand, not letting her go."
- "I could say, 'No, you can get hurt,' and take her inside."
- "I could not let her play alone in an unfenced yard."

3. Evaluate the ideas.

- *Spanking:*

"Spanking would be hurting her to teach her not to get hurt. That doesn't make sense. She might be afraid to do it again because she won't want to get spanked, but she won't hesitate when she thinks I cannot see."

- *Yelling:*

"Yelling at her doesn't make sense because she probably won't understand what it's all about."

- *Firmness:*

"Taking her firmly by the hand, taking her inside, or only allowing her to play in a fenced-in area all make sense."

Let's see how these solutions fit into our chart.

Consequence	Make Sense?	Preserve Dignity?	Make Accountable?
Spank	no	no	no
Yell	no	no	no
Say no, hold	yes	yes	yes
Say no, remove	yes	yes	yes
Restrict	yes	yes	yes

4. Select an idea.

The only way to prevent her from doing it again is to hold her hand or let her play only in a fenced-in yard. Remember the age of the child when choosing a consequence. Two-year-olds cannot be responsible for their own safety. We adults must protect them from harm while at the same time explaining to them why they are being restricted.

5. Try out the idea.

"I'll hold Jenna's hand or stay within arm's reach unless we're in a fenced-in area."

6. Evaluate effectiveness.

"I feel much better, and Jenna is safe."

7. Decide.

"It works. Jenna is not running out into the street."

III. Problem Solving: Preventing Future Problems

1. State the problem.
"How can I keep Jenna from running into the street?"

2. Brainstorm ideas.
+ I can hold Jenna's hand all the time.
+ I can stay within arm's reach when not in a fenced-in yard.
+ I can restrict her to the fenced-in yard.

3. Evaluate the ideas.
+ *Hold hand:*
"Sometimes that's possible, but other times, I may have to give her some space."
+ *Stay close by:*
"That seems possible to do, but I can't take my eye off her for a second."
+ *Stay in fenced yard:*
"This isn't always possible."

4. Select an idea.
Sometimes, particularly in the case of young children, we do not need to enforce consequences but only to design preventive measures. For example, if a three-year-old plays with matches, it is sufficient to place them out of reach. However, merely placing alcohol out of the reach of a sixteen-year-old would not be enough.

In this case, Mom must use whatever measures are appropriate for the situation—hand-holding, staying nearby, or fences. Two-year-olds cannot be responsible for their own safety. Why worry about consequences when prevention works best?

Example: Eight-year-old Matt hits people when he gets angry at them.

I. Problem Solving: Figuring Out the Cause

1. State the problem.
Why does Matt hit when he is angry?

2. Brainstorm ideas.
- He does not know how else to express his emotions.
- He is just a mean person.

3. Evaluate the ideas.
Matt may not know how to express his anger. He isn't just a mean person; at times he can be very kind. He only hits when he is extremely angry.

4. Select an idea.
Therefore, Matt probably hits when he is angry because he does not know what else to do.

II. Problem Solving: Preventing Future Problems
We will discuss this on page 135.

III. Problem Solving: Selecting Appropriate Consequences

1. State the problem.
What consequence will follow Matt's hurting other people when he is angry, if he does this again?

2. Brainstorm ideas.
- Spank him.
- Yell at him.

♦ Send him to time-out.
♦ Tell the other children to hit him back.

3. Evaluate the ideas.
   ♦ *Spank:*
   Spanking him doesn't make sense because it's hurting him to get him to stop hurting other people. It might make him afraid to hit anyone again.
   ♦ *Yell:*
   Yelling at him doesn't make sense because he probably won't even listen and he'll just keep on hitting.
   ♦ *Time-out:*
   Sending him to time-out makes sense because if he doesn't know how to behave around people, then he should not be with them.
   ♦ *Other children hit back:*
   It doesn't make sense to tell the other kids that it is okay to hit. Also, having the other kids hit him back means that he will be more likely to hit them.

4. Select an idea.
   The best solution, then, is to put him in a time-out area where he is away from the other children.

III. Problem Solving: Preventing Future Problems
   We will discuss this on page 135.

Example: One Saturday night, sixteen-year-old Alice came home one hour after her curfew.

I. Problem Solving: Figuring Out the Case

1. State the problem.
Why was Alice late?

2. Brainstorm ideas.
In this case it is important to listen to Alice to understand why she came home late. Perhaps she has a perfectly reasonable explanation. Among the reasons that may go through your mind are:

- She forgot to check the time.
- She had too much to drink.
- Her car broke down.
- She couldn't find a safe ride home.

3. Evaluate and select an idea.
Try to make it comfortable for Alice to tell you the truth and then accept what she says. In this case, let us suppose that Alice claimed to have lost track of time.

II. Problem Solving: Preventing Future Problems
We will discuss this on page 136.

III. Problem Solving: Selecting Appropriate Consequences

1. State the problem.
What would be a consequence for Alice coming home one hour after her curfew?

2. Brainstorm ideas.
- "Not let her go out for a month."
- "Not let her go out for one weekend."
- "Take away her telephone."

+ "Take away her car."
+ "Have her do one hour of work for me to compensate for my hour of worry."

3 & 4. Evaluate and select an idea.

Beware of consequences that go on and on or are too harsh. "It doesn't make sense to take away her phone or her car. It does make sense to keep her home, but one weekend is probably enough. It also makes sense to have her do one hour of work for me, but I think it will make more of an impression for her to stay home one weekend."

5. Try out the idea.

Alice stays home for one weekend and does not go out with her friends.

6. Evaluate effectiveness.

Alice continues to stay out late.

7. Decide.

Return to either steps #1, #2, or #3.

THE THREE R'S OF PREVENTION

By the time children are around five years old, we can involve them in preventive problem solving. With our guidance, they can figure out what to do to help themselves not misbehave again. There are actually three stages (the three "R"s) for achieving this long-term behavior change: recognition, remorse, and resolve.

Recognition

Before a problem can be solved, one must recognize that a problem exists. This recognition is achieved during the first problem-solving step, "stating the problem." Sometimes children will be aware on their own that a problem exists while other times, we might have to make them aware. For example, in Matt's case (page 130), "I notice that when you get angry, you start to hit people" might be the opener that leads to "What can you do instead of hitting when you are very angry?"

Remorse

Only if we feel remorse about what we have done will we be willing to change. Having remorse means having a conscience. There are two facets to remorse: (1) understanding the negative impact of our actions on others and (2) understanding the negative impact of our actions on ourselves. For Matt, it would mean acknowledging that hitting hurts others and thus is unacceptable and that children won't want to be around him if he hits.

It is important that remorse be achieved through a calm, matter-of-fact discussion. That means no lectures, no guilt trips, no harangues. If our children are made to feel hopelessly bad about themselves or if they feel threatened, they will be less likely to be open to change.

Resolve

Changing behavior means resolving to do so by having a specific plan of action. "The next time this situation arises I will———— instead." Resolve requires that the child must be involved in both brainstorming and in choosing the solution. In Matt's case, he could come up with several ideas as to what he could do instead of hitting when he is angry. Then, by evaluating each idea, he could choose the idea that he thinks will work best for him. Matt might need some help with this process. We can throw in a few suggestions of our own and even help him evaluate each suggestion. But, by involving Matt in the process and not making all the decisions ourselves, we make it likely that he will own the solution and resolve to change.

Keeping the three "R"s of recognition, remorse, and resolve in mind as we deal with discipline problems can guide us to long-lasting successful solutions.

Now, let's look at the preventive problem-solving steps for Matt and Alice.

Problem Solving: Preventing Future Problems

Matt

1. State the problem.

   What can Matt do besides hit when he is very angry?

2. Brainstorm ideas.
   * Tell Matt that it's not right to hit when you're angry.
   * Help Matt figure out what else he can do when he is angry.

3. Evaluate the ideas.

   Just telling Matt not to hit isn't going to work because he doesn't know what else to do. If he figures out what else to do, then maybe he'll stop. In this case, the solution would be to help Matt think up what he *can* do when he's angry. Among his ideas might be to count to ten, punch a punching bag, play with Play-Doh, take a walk, listen to music . . . whatever works best to get him to cool off so that he can then talk about how he feels is the one he should choose. Different approaches work for different people, and only Matt knows what will work best for him. You may have to start him off with ideas.

4. Select an idea.

   Matt decides to count backward from ten when he starts to feel very angry.

5. Try out the idea.

Matt counted backward from ten when he was angry.

6. Evaluate effectiveness.

He stopped hitting when angry.

7. Decide.

The problem is solved. No further action necessary. If the counting didn't work for Matt, then he would have to return to step #3 and figure out something else to calm himself down.

Alice

1. State the problem.

How can Alice be helped not to lose track of time and be late?

2. Brainstorm ideas (Alice can do this by herself or together with you).

- Wear a watch with a timer.
- Ask a friend to remind her.
- Tie a string around her finger to remind her to check the time.
- Have her parents call or beep her to remind her.

3 & 4. Evaluate and select an idea.

Certainly Alice would not want her parents calling to remind her, so she decided to wear a watch that would beep thirty minutes before her curfew.

5. Try out the idea.

Alice wears her watch when she goes out.

6. Evaluate effectiveness.

She was not late again.

7. Decide.

The problem is solved. If this did not work for Alice then she would have to go back to step #3 and figure out what else she could do so that she would remember to come home on time.

With practice, this problem solving will come naturally to you. Your children will learn how to do it by following your example. As children get older, they can be involved in all three kinds of problem solving—figuring out why, preventing the problem from happening again, and setting consequences. Sometimes, it might be helpful for you and your children to either talk through or write out a contract for how they can prevent the problem from recurring.

SAMPLE CONTRACT
Date:
This is what happened:
This is why it happened:
It was a problem because:
Effect on others:
Effect on me:
Here are some ways I can help it from not happening again:
This is what I choose to do so it won't happen again:

This contract can combine both why the child thinks the problem happened and how he thinks he can stop it from resurfacing.

After a week or two, go back to the contract and see if it's working. If it is, great. If it isn't, do some more problem solving until the problem is solved.

Summary

Problem solving is a way of thinking that helps us keep our cool and plan for how we will deal with misbehavior. It helps us not to fly off the handle and then be sorry later. We don't have to solve every problem on the spot. We can take time to figure out what to do. As we practice this approach, we will need less and less time to decide what we will do. It's important that our children see us thinking before we act. After all, isn't that what we're trying to get them to do?

SUMMARY OF MAIN POINTS

- Problem solving can help us parents determine our course of action when it comes to discipline issues.

- Problem solving can be used as a tool for figuring out what caused misbehavior.

- Problem solving can be used as a tool for preventing future misbehavior.

- Problem solving can be used as a tool for selecting appropriate consequences.

- Problem solving is a tool that can be useful for many aspects of our lives.

- Children can be involved in the problem-solving process.

- The three "R"s for achieving long-term behavior change are recognition, remorse, and resolve.

CHAPTER NINE

What to Do When Children Fight

Mrs. Jones had two cupcakes, one chocolate and one vanilla. She promised her two children that the child who cleaned up his/her room first would get first choice of cupcakes. Kelly finished first. "Okay Kelly!" exclaimed Mom. "You get to choose first." Kelly responded, "No, I want to wait and see which one Eric chooses, and that's the one I want!"

Among the frantic pleas of parents are: "How do I stop my kids from fighting with each other?" "How do I remain calm, cool, and collected when three young children are fighting and screaming and all I want to do is scream back at them?" "I know my kids love each other, but why do they keep arguing and bickering with each other all the time?" "I can't stand the noise when my kids start fighting. I feel like I'm going crazy." "What can I do about their fighting? I've tried everything—ignoring them, punishing them, sending them to time-out." "I'm so afraid they'll hurt each other when they fight."

Sibling rivalry has been going on ever since the first two siblings, Cain and Abel, arrived on this earth. Fighting, disagreeing, and arguing come with the territory of having a sibling—it's hard to share your parents, your home, and your possessions with another child. Anytime people of different sizes, temperaments, interests, and ages are thrown together, there is bound to be friction.

In addition, siblings are often the safest target onto which a child can unleash his or her frustration and resentment. It is normal at times for a child to feel frustrated and resentful. It is sometimes hard to be a child. Adults order children around: "Do this, do that, don't do this, don't do that." If children express their anger at their parents or teachers, what might happen? They might get punished. Many children feel resentful but know that they will get in trouble if they snap back at their parents or teachers or refuse to do what they are told. They often let out their anger on siblings, who don't have the power and authority of adults.

It is normal for children to have some conflict with friends over possessions or other friends, but if they let out their anger on their companions, they might lose them. Kids must be careful about letting out all their resentment on their friends if they want to keep them. But they can never lose their brothers and sisters. Siblings are a captive audience. Therefore, they can be a safe outlet for venting frustration and resentment.

Do you ever get concerned that you failed as a parent because even after you've told your children over and over not to fight, they still persist in fighting? We have not failed as parents if our children fight. Sibling rivalry is a perfectly normal by-product of family life. In fact, siblings can reap advantages from their skirmishes with their brothers and sisters. Some advantages are:

♦ **Self-expression:** "That's my doll and you must ask me before you play with it." "He sat in the front seat yesterday.

Today it's my turn." By speaking up for themselves at home, siblings can learn how to stand up for themselves in the world and how to protect their own interests.

◆ **Conflict resolution:** "You broke my game. How will you pay me back?" "Even though you got there first, it's my turn." Siblings can learn how to negotiate and resolve conflicts.

◆ **Tolerance:** Unlike with friends, siblings cannot discontinue their relationship just because they have an argument. Siblings learn that even though they might have a conflict with someone, they can continue living side by side with that person.

Unfortunately, only children do not have these advantages.

What about the disadvantages of sibling rivalry? Some adults bear very deep scars, both physical and emotional, from their fights with their siblings. "My brother always called me Dumbo because of my big ears. I always keep my hair long to cover them." "I can't stand bossy people. They remind me of my older sister." "Teachers always kept reminding me how smart my sister was in math. To this day I hate to do math." "I hate the word *crazy*. That's what my sister called me. I bristle every time I hear that word."

Sibling rivalry is normal, and if anyone tells you that their children don't have any rivalry, be *very* suspicious. Let's face it. We cannot eliminate sibling rivalry completely, nor should we want to. Instead, we can try to keep it at a manageable level so that our children will have happier, less stressful childhoods and so that they will not carry physical and emotional scars with them into adulthood. Then we can use outbreaks of sibling rivalry as opportunities for teaching nonhurtful self-expression, conflict resolution, and tolerance.

How can we parents keep sibling rivalry from getting out of

hand? First of all, we can try to eliminate or minimize any avoidable sources of sibling rivalry. Second, when conflicts arise, we can use the problem-solving model so that we don't take sides and interfere but instead teach our children how to solve their disputes constructively and independently.

SIBLING RIVALRY: WHAT WE CAN DO

Jealousy is a major source of sibling rivalry. Children compete with each other for their parents' attention. Siblings also struggle for the equal distribution of privileges among themselves, and they vie with each other for possessions.

But why add fuel to the fire? As parents, we can worsen the rivalry. "Why are you so jealous?" "You're too big for that." "She needs help, but you can do it by yourself." "You have to set an example." "You're selfish." These are negative comments that make this parent-sharing that much harder and pave the road for sibling rivalry. Let's look at how we as parents can keep sibling rivalry to a tolerable level.

Preventing Some Sibling Fights: Competition for Attention

There's only so much of the parental pie to go around. It's inevitable that brothers and sisters will sometimes have to compete with each other for their parents' attention. There are times when one child will feel left out because we need to take care of her sibling. If one child consistently receives special attention because of age, a disability, or a talent, then the sibling rivalry may be even more intense. The other siblings will try to demand their fair share.

Sometimes we show favoritism to children because they share a common interest with us. A dad who is an athlete may be attracted to the child that shows an interest in athletics. Dad and child may want to spend more time together because of their common interest. It's normal that some children are a better "fit" with us in terms of interests, personality, and temperament.

Sometimes children experience self-imposed competition, particularly if they're less than two years apart. "Why can't I read if she can?" "I'll learn how to ride a bike before she does."

If you find that one child is acting very jealous or resentful of another and constantly demanding your attention, ask yourself if you are showing favoritism, for whatever reason. If you are, and there is no compelling reason for doing so, maybe you *are* being unfair. Try to evaluate the situation, listen to your children's complaints, and change your behavior. It's okay to let them know that we make mistakes. That's one way we can teach them how to admit their own mistakes.

Often, however, we are justified in showing what a sibling views as favoritism. Favoritism can be justified for reasons of age— "She's younger; she needs more help cleaning her room," or "He's too young to have to do the dishes"—or disability—"She's too fragile to help out." We can explain this to our children at their level, but children do not have the same sense of fairness and understanding as do adults. They may be unable to understand the logic of our reasoning, or they may understand the logic but emotionally still feel neglected and left out.

If you are justifiably showing favoritism, or even if you do not think you are showing favoritism, some remedies might be:

• Try to listen and acknowledge this child's feelings. Encourage the child to verbalize his or her strong feelings. "It's hard to share with the new baby." "That gets you very angry when you have friends over and your sister keeps knocking at your door." Even if you cannot give the child attention on the spot, you can acknowledge his feelings. When someone acknowledges our feelings, we feel validated. Just that acknowledgment alone may be enough to satisfy the child because you're on the same wavelength. "She understands me. She's not disagreeing with me. I don't have to fight with her."

• Try to include the resentful or hurt child. To help this child not feel so left out, find ways to include him in your activities. Perhaps go to the younger child's room with the older child and make cleaning up together a game. Or ask the older child to help you figure out how you can divide up the dishwashing responsibilities.

• Try to pay some more attention in general to the needy child to balance the extra attention you have to give to the sibling. Try to spend some extra private time with this child, even just reading a book or taking a walk.

When a child seeks attention, try to find an acceptable way to provide this attention. Often this is the easiest and best solution.

If you just ignore this child, it's 99 percent guaranteed that he'll try some other way to get your attention, and it most likely won't be very acceptable to you. Perhaps you will find your best lipstick used for a drawing on the mirror, a radio turned up so loud that the walls are shaking, or that this child is developing learning problems in school. In children's eyes, negative attention is better than no attention at all.

If you tell this child that it's tough, and he'll just have to accept the situation, he'll most likely become angry and resentful. At some later point, he may vent this hostility on either you or the sibling. He may break the sibling's toy, refuse to help out when needed, or find some other way to get back at you for denying his feelings, especially when you're not around.

Preventing Some Sibling Fights: Competition for Privileges

"Why can't I go to the mall alone? You let Jenny go!" "Why can't I have chocolate milk? Carlos did!" "When I was her age, you never let me do that." "How come she can stay up later than I can?" When children live in the same house, it is natural that they will compare themselves to each other. They want to be sure they're getting their fair share of privileges. They often compete for privileges just as they do for attention. If your children complain, try to ask yourself *why* you are allowing different privileges for different children.

First, if you can't justify your behavior, admit it and adjust accordingly. Sometimes we don't realize that we're not being fair until our children point it out. Sometimes we forget to adjust our privileges and expectations to the growing capabilities of our children. When children first start school, they may not be able to ride a bike to school, but as they mature, it may be appropriate. You may have let your older child ride his bike to school at a certain age but denied the same privilege when the younger one reached this age. Maybe you think of the younger one as your baby. After the younger child brings this to your attention, however, you can say, "You have a point. You are indeed old enough now to ride your bike to school."

Second, if you think your reasons are justified, then explain them to your child. Age, environmental circumstances, and development all are factors that determine privileges. "Jenny is older. It is unsafe for children your age to go to the mall alone." "He can have a treat because he hasn't had one yet today." "You were my first child. I was stricter because I did not have the experience."

Once again, your child may not be able to process this reason emotionally. To help him accept the situation without resenting you or the other child, try to acknowledge his feelings. "It is hard sometimes being the youngest. Everyone seems to do so much more than you." Perhaps spend some extra time with him, such as doing something special while the older child is at the mall. Perhaps you can find an appropriate substitute privilege for him, such as going to his favorite store with him. I'm sure you can think of many other approaches along these lines that will work for you.

Preventing Some Sibling Fights: Competition for Possessions

"It's mine." "No. It's mine. I got it first." These kinds of fights can drive parents crazy. The name-calling and bickering are most annoying, and it's nerve-racking to be interrupted from work or relaxation to settle fights.

Some of these fights can be eliminated with the following suggestions. Nevertheless, some will still occur. We will discuss later how problem solving and conflict resolution are extremely effective tools for dealing with them. However, some suggestions for preventing fights over possessions from even occurring are:

- Be very clear about which possessions belong to which person—toys, clothes, books—and which are family possessions.

- Establish procedures for borrowing someone else's possessions. How does one ask permission? What happens if the owner is not home? Does the parent have the right to grant permission in that case?

- Establish procedures for a situation where the possession is dirtied or ruined. The borrower must return the object in its original condition or make restitution whenever possible.

- Be sure that you, the parent, also respect the rules for borrowing.

Intervening When Siblings Fight

Problem solving (see chapter 8) can be used in two different ways to help us deal with sibling rivalry. It can help us parents figure out how to handle some situations when we are caught up in them, and it can help us guide our children when they are fighting with each other.

Problem Solving for Constructive Approaches to Sibling Rivalry

Sometimes we get into conflicts with our children over sibling rivalry, and problem solving can help us figure out how we can avoid a major discipline problem. In this case, we do the problem solving ourselves. (Again, while this approach may seem awkward at first, parents have found that it quickly becomes more natural.)

Example 1.

It's so tempting to do just what Mommy did here:

(Setting: Brad, age three, and Mike, age eight, are home with their mother on a Saturday afternoon)

BRAD: *Read to me, read to me, Mommy!*
MOMMY: *Okay. Bring me your favorite book.*
BRAD: *Here it is.*
MIKE: *That's not fair. You're reading him books and you're not doing anything with me.*
MOMMY: *Well, you're bigger, Mike, so you can do things for yourself. Besides, you know how to read, and he doesn't.*
BRAD: *Yeah, you know how to read, Mike, and I don't.*
MIKE: *You keep out of this, Brad. I'm not talking to you.*
MOMMY: *Well, he happens to be right.*
MIKE: *No, he's not. It's not fair.*
MOMMY: *I think it's very fair because you can read to yourself.*

MIKE: *But I don't feel like reading. I want you to do something with me.*

MOMMY: *You're just being selfish.*

MIKE: *No, I'm not.*

MOMMY: *Yes, you are.*

MIKE: *You know what I'm going to do, Mommy?*

MOMMY: *What are you going to do?*

MIKE: *I'm going to keep interrupting you so he can't hear the story. So there!*

Mike certainly manipulated this situation so that he felt victorious. What a discipline disaster for Mommy. Let's look at how problem solving could have helped Mommy figure out a constructive approach to this situation:

Step 1. She states the problem.
"How can I read and give attention to Brad without having Mike get jealous and interrupt us?"

Step 2. She brainstorms all the solutions she can think of for this problem.
(Below are some examples of the solutions many parents have suggested.)

"Just tell him it's too bad, let him feel jealous; don't spoil him."

"Don't read a book to anyone."

"Send Mike to his room or time-out."

"Have Mike help me read the book or turn the pages."

"Acknowledge that it's hard to wait, but after I read this book, I'll read a book to him."

"Punish Mike. Don't let him go out to play."

Step 3. Evaluate the solutions.
+ *Too bad:*
"Leaving him to feel jealous could make all three of us miserable. He might keep annoying us and will be hurt, angry, and very resentful of his brother."
+ *Don't read to anyone:*
"Why punish Brad?"
+ *Send to time-out:*
"He might feel even more left out that way."
+ *Have Mike help:*
"This could work well."
+ *Acknowledge Mike's feelings and read later:*
"This could also work."
+ *Punish:*
"Punishing Mike for feeling jealous is only going to make him resentful of both me and Brad. This creates fertile ground for fights between siblings."

Step 4. Select a solution.
In this case, either the fourth or fifth solution could be selected. You can probably think up other acceptable solutions as well. Then Mom could proceed to steps # 5, # 6, and # 7.

Example 2: Copy cat.
Let's look at another familiar situation with Anna, ten years old, and Beth, eight years old.

MOM: *How do you like this restaurant, kids?*
ANNA: *I like it.*
BETH: *I like it.*
ANNA: *You don't have to copy everything I say.*
BETH: *I can if I want to.*
MOM: *Please, kids, stop your bickering. Let's try to have a*

peaceful lunch here in this nice restaurant. What would you like, girls? Who's ready to order?

ANNA: *I am. I want a hamburger with ketchup, and I want some french fries and a Coke.*

MOM: *How about you, Beth?*

BETH: *I want a hamburger with ketchup, some french fries, and a Coke.*

ANNA: *Stop copying me! Mom, I want Beth to stop copying me. I don't want her to order the same thing.*

MOM: *Why not?*

ANNA: *Because I don't like it. I don't like her to copy me. She can order something different.*

BETH: *No, I want a hamburger with ketchup, some french fries, and a Coke.*

ANNA: *Then I'll order something different.*

MOM: *Now, that's silly. Tell me, exactly what difference does it make if you both have the same orders?*

ANNA: *Because she's always copying me, and I don't like it.*

MOM: *That's ridiculous. I'm putting in your orders right now.*

ANNA: *But if she has the same, I'm telling you I'm not going to eat it.*

MOM: *Okay then, let's not bother to order anything. We'll go home and have a peanut butter sandwich. Come on, let's go, I'm not putting up with this foolishness!*

Mom's solution made everyone miserable. A pleasant outing was ruined for them all. Let's examine how Mom could have used the problem-solving process herself to figure out a better solution:

Step 1. To herself, Mom could state the problem. "Beth is copying Anna. Anna wants Beth to stop. How can I get them both to stop so we can have a peaceful lunch?"

Step 2. Here are some solutions that Mom might have come up with brainstorming:

A. "We'll leave the restaurant."

B. "I'll tell Anna that she doesn't have to eat if she doesn't want to."

C. "I'll explain to Anna that younger children copy people they look up to."

D. "I'll allow Anna to order something else."

E. "I'll acknowledge to Anna that she must be feeling frustrated, but that's what younger children do sometimes."

F. "I'll tell Beth to stop copying. She can order the same food, but she must stop mimicking Anna's words."

G. "I'll have Anna mimic Beth back."

Step 3. There's no one correct solution. Mom would have to evaluate all the solutions to see which would turn out most favorably for them and allow them to enjoy their meal in the restaurant. She might think:

A. "This will satisfy no one."

B. "Telling Anna that she doesn't have to eat is actually punishing her. What would happen if she chose not to eat? She would be miserable and probably so would everyone else."

C. "This might work for Anna. It may make her feel important."

D. "Why not? It's everyone's time out. This is not the time to be teaching Anna a lesson and punishing her. When someone copies you, it often is annoying."

E. "Sometimes just acknowledging a child's feelings is enough to satisfy the child. They just want to be heard. This might work for Anna, but I think she's too upset."

F. "Why not ask Beth to stop? It's certainly appropriate to tell a child not to do something that offends others."

G. "Telling Anna to copy Beth only escalates the problem and
could end up with a screaming competition."

Certainly, on the spot, Mom would not have time to
think up all these solutions, but she could come up with
three or four.

Step 4. No one can tell Mom which of the acceptable solutions (C, D, E, F) would work for her particular children.
She has to decide for herself. The same is true for you. You
may be able to think up even better solutions. Just remember, when you are in a situation where you have to think
up the solution, try to find a solution that ends up peacefully.

PROBLEM SOLVING FOR CONFLICT RESOLUTION

Do you ever feel like a referee between your children? You feel
like you have to stand there, call the shots, and give the orders to
settle fights. Usually, at least one of the children ends up dissatis-
fied with the results. Sometimes it's very tempting to take sides.
And usually, we take the side of the one who calls us for help.
"Mom, Johnny's hitting me." "Johnny, why are you hitting your
sister?"

But the best approach for both us and our kids when they fight
with each other and we are not part of the scene until someone
comes screaming to us for help is to place the problem solving
right where it belongs—in the hands of the quarreling children.
Here is where the problem-solving technique described in chapter
8 can take a tremendous burden off us parents. The basic steps in
using problem solving to deal with conflicts between people are:

1. State the problem:
   a. Cool off if everyone is too heated to discuss rationally.
   b. Each person listens to the other person tell his or her

side of the story, including how he or she feels about the situation and how they think the other person feels (see chapter 5 for suggestions of how to express feelings non-hurtfully).

c. Together they try to figure out what their problem is.

2. **Together brainstorm** as many solutions as they can think of. Remember, at this stage the solutions don't have to be particularly good nor do they have to be acceptable to both parties at this point. Quantity, not quality, is the goal.

3. **Together evaluate** all the solutions and discuss which ones are acceptable to both parties. If there aren't any acceptable ones, go back to step two and think of some more.

4. **Choose a solution** that both parties agree on.

5. **Try out the solution.**

6. **& 7. If it works,** keep it up, and if it doesn't, go back and figure out another solution.

At first we may have to be the mediators, and this may take a little extra time. We may have to take our children step by step through the problem-solving process—guiding them in stating the problem, brainstorming solutions with them, and helping them select a feasible solution. But after a few times with you as their mediator, your kids will be able to follow these steps on their own. Aaah, what a pleasure it will be when they stop coming to you to settle every little spat! Surely, they'll need your help once in a while, but helping kids with problem solving is far easier to do than playing Solomon. Yes, problem solving does take time. But parents who have used it are so thankful because it takes less and less time and energy with practice.

Example 3: Fights.

Let's look at how problem solving could have helped with this. Here's an all-too-common situation: Father is watching a ball game on TV. Stephen and Melissa are on the other side of the room.

STEPHEN: *Melissa, give me my ball.*

MELISSA: *No, I want to play with it.*

STEPHEN: *Well, it's mine, and I need it right away. My friends are waiting for me outside.*

MELISSA: (pouting) *I don't care, I'm not going to give it to you.* (teasing) *Besides, you know what Daddy says about sharing.*

STEPHEN: *Now, you give it to me or I'll . . .* (grabbing it)

MELISSA: (screaming) *Daddy, Daddy, Daddy!*

FATHER: (getting up, very angry) *Now what's going on here? What's all this commotion? Can't I relax for a few minutes in peace? What are you two fighting about again?*

MELISSA: (crying) *He's selfish. He isn't sharing.*

STEPHEN: *But she took my ball and I want it. The guys are waiting outside for me to play with them.*

MELISSA: (pouting) *Well, I had it first.*

STEPHEN: *It's mine, and I need it now.*

FATHER: (sternly) *Now, look here, Stephen, you're bigger than she is. You ought to know better. Go find something else to play with and let her have it.*

STEPHEN: (helplessly) *But, Dad, it's my ball, and I need it.*

FATHER: (very sternly) *Oh, stop your arguing. Go along and act your age!*

What was the end result here? Melissa got her way because she was younger. What does this teach Melissa? Probably that she can whine and use her family position as a bargaining chip to get whatever she wants. Stephen was probably furious at both his father and his sister. After all, the solution wasn't fair to him, and his point of view wasn't even heard. The father took the whole burden of solving the problem onto himself and probably fumed about it all the while that he watched TV. It may have seemed like the easy way out, but look at the price everyone paid. Let's look at how Melissa and Stephen's father could have used the problem-solving technique:

At the point where the father is called in, the following conversation could have taken place:

FATHER: *Now what's going on here? I want each of you to take turns and tell me what's the problem. Okay, Melissa, you go first. Now, remember, don't interrupt each other. You'll each have a chance to tell your story.*

MELISSA: *I was playing with the ball, and Stephen came over and took it from me.*

FATHER: *How did you feel, Melissa?*

MELISSA: *I was mad. I was having fun.*

FATHER: *Okay, son, now you tell us.*

STEPHEN: *My friends and I were going to play ball, so I needed my ball. Melissa was playing with it and she wouldn't give it to me, even though it was my ball.*

FATHER: *How did you feel, Stephen?*

STEPHEN: *I was nervous and rushed. I was afraid my friends would leave without me.*

FATHER: *I see, kids, so the problem is that you both want to play with the ball at the same time?* (statement of the problem)

STEPHEN AND MELISSA TOGETHER: *Yes.*

FATHER: *What ideas do you two have for solving this problem?* (brainstorming)

Together, the children and their father come up with the following ideas:

"Stephen will get the ball because it's his."

"Melissa will get the ball because she had it first."

"Cut the ball in half."

"Find another ball for Melissa or Stephen."

"Find another toy for Melissa."

"Melissa could join Stephen and his friends."

"Stephen could promise Melissa the ball for the next day."

"Stephen could lend Melissa another one of his toys."

"Melissa could call up a friend to play."

After the brainstorming, Melissa, Stephen, and their father can look over the suggestions, evaluate each of them, and figure out which one they can all agree upon. It's unlikely that the first three suggestions will be acceptable to all of them. However, the other suggestions might work, depending on the situation. Only Stephen, Melissa, and their father know which solution would work best for their particular circumstances. Some of these ideas might work for you in a similar situation. You might find other solutions that would work even better. But the problem-solving approach works for all situations—brainstorms solutions and then pick the one you all think will work best.

After the solution is picked, Stephen and Melissa should go off to try it out, and their father will, we hope, go back to enjoying the television. If the fight stops, the problem is solved. If the children are fighting again in five minutes, they need to go through the steps again and find a new solution that will stop them from fighting.

Yes, this does take time. Bringing up children properly, teaching them self-control and self-discipline, is a time-consuming project. However, once kids get the hang of this kind of approach, it takes less and less time. Just think of the time and energy you'll save by not having to break up fights yourself.

Example 4: Tattletale.

Tattletales can drive us crazy. But the way we address their complaints can determine whether they keep on tattling or solve their own problems:

JULIA: *Mom, Connor's always fighting with me.*
MOM: *So fight back.*
JULIA: *I can't. He's too big.*
MOM: *So walk away.*
JULIA: *I can't. He chases me.*
MOM: *So, go to your room.*
JULIA: *He comes in there, too.*
MOM: *So what do you want me to do?*
JULIA: *I want you to tell him to stop fighting with me.*
MOM: *The next time he fights with you, come and tell me, and I'll put a stop to it. Remember, just tell me.*
A few minutes later, Julia runs up.
JULIA: (screaming) *Mom, Mom, Connor's after me! He's going to hit me!*
MOM: *Stop being a tattletale.*

What are some of the problems here?

1. Mom keeps coming up with the solutions rather than Julia.

2. Mom does not know if Connor is teasing Julia or not.

3. Mom does not know if Julia is just tattling to get Connor in trouble with Mom.

4. Mom actually encouraged Julia to tell her and then calls her a tattletale when she does.

See chapter 11 for a discussion of what makes children tattle.

Mom could have saved the whole family a great deal of aggravation by taking the problem-solving approach. She could have remained neutral by not taking sides, brought the two children together, and let each of them tell his or her side of the story. "Okay, Julia, tell me what happened and how you were feeling." "Now, Connor, you tell what happened and how you were feeling." After that, Mom could help Connor and Julia brainstorm ideas to stop the bickering. Then together they could choose the solution to the bickering that would be acceptable to all of them. Thus, the responsibility for solving the problem would be placed in the hands of those to whom it rightfully belonged—the children. The appeal of tattling would be removed because Julia would learn that Mom is not going to solve the problem for her. Connor would also have to own up to his actions.

Example 5: Fights that pull our strings.

Some of our children's fights drive us crazy because they dredge up unpleasant memories from our own childhoods (see chapter 6). Does it drive you crazy when kids tattle on each other? Perhaps you remember when your younger brother or sister tattled on you. Do you see red when your older child seems to be picking on your younger child? Does it remind you of when your older sibling picked on you? Do you explode when one child teases and calls another names? Do you remember hurtful names that stuck to you?

It's sometimes difficult not to get caught up in our own emotions, but we must be especially careful in situations like these not to let our emotional baggage exacerbate the problem. The problem-solving approach can help you separate yourself from the situation, step back, take a deep breath, and try to resolve the conflict without overpersonalizing and without getting overwrought. The key is to separate our own issues from the issues at hand.

Kristen comes screaming into the kitchen, "Mom, Dan called

me fat. I'm not fat, am I? Get him to stop. It's not fair." Mom, who was a bit plump herself as a child, still bears the scars of being teased and called names like "fatty" and "butterball." When Kristen tells her that Dan called his sister fat, Mom flies into a rage. "Dan, get over here right this minute. What right do you have to call your sister fat? Look what you're doing to her. Why are you so mean?"

Wouldn't they all be better off if Mom could stop for a minute, call Dan into the room, and then hear out both children?

MOM: *Dan, come in here now, please.*

DAN: *It's not my fault. You should hear what she said to me.*

MOM: *Settle down, and let me hear each of you, one at a time.*

DAN: *We were playing cards, and she started cheating. I told her she was cheating, and she threw down all the cards and swore at me and told me I was a poor sport. So I told her she was a big fat liar and that she really was cheating.*

MOM: *How did you feel?*

DAN: *I was really furious because I know she was cheating, but I didn't mean to call her fat, just a big fat liar. That's different.*

MOM: *Okay, Kristen, let's hear your side.*

KRISTEN: *We were playing cards, and all of a sudden he said I was cheating. I wasn't, so I got mad and threw down the cards. He called me a big fat liar.*

MOM: *How did you feel?*

KRISTEN: *I know I'm fat, he doesn't have to tell me. He only makes me feel worse. Besides, what does my being fat have to do with that old game anyway?*

MOM: *What do you two think the problem is?*

DAN: *I called her a fat liar and all she heard was the word fat. I guess I shouldn't have used the word fat—that was pretty mean.*

KRISTEN: *Okay. I'm sorry, too. I didn't mean to cheat, but maybe it seemed that way.*

MOM: *What do you think you can do the next time to prevent something like this from happening?*

The next step for the children would be to brainstorm solutions. "Not play cards together," "Have clear rules for playing," etc. If we can separate, take a deep breath, calm down before we react, and put problem solving into action, we can prevent ourselves from adding our own personal fuel to the flames of sibling rivalry.

Example 6: Resolving miscommunication through problem solving.

It's not always necessary to complete all the steps of problem solving. Sometimes when children just take the time to hear each other out (step #1), they realize that they just misunderstood each other, and the problem is resolved.

Steam was rising from the group of third graders as I entered my student teacher's classroom. Two groups of girls seemed to be on the verge of coming to blows with each other. "What's the problem?" I asked, and then let the central figure in each group tell her side of the story:

ELLEN: *A few weeks ago I brought a foreign coin to school, and Jonathan took it, so today I took his quarter. The teacher told me to give it back, and then she* (pointing to Maya) *told me to give it back.*

ME: *How did you feel?*

ELLEN: *Hurt. She was siding with the teacher, and I know I was right.*

ME: *Okay, Maya, now you tell us what happened.*

MAYA: *Jonathan did take her coin, and so she took his quarter. When the teacher told her to give back the quarter, I told her she'd better.*

ME: *How did you feel?*

MAYA: *Worried because I thought she'd get in big trouble with the teacher.*

ME: *Oh, so, Ellen, you were upset because you thought your friend was going against you in siding with the teacher, and Maya, you were upset because you were worried about your friend getting in trouble with the teacher?*

MAYA AND ELLEN: *Yes.*

ME: *So you were fighting because you both cared so much about your friendship?* (statement of the problem)

The girls nodded their heads; both they and their cohorts who had been taking sides skipped off to play. Should they be punished for fighting? Why? They didn't do any harm to each other. Should they have to go through all the problem-solving steps? Why bother? The problem of miscommunication was solved. Certainly not all of children's conflicts will disappear just by opening up the lines of communication, but many will with just this first problem-solving step.

Summary

Conflict in and of itself is not bad. We often grow and learn from our disagreements. First, hearing another person's point of view may teach us something we have never known before. Second, when we have to put our ideas into words and explain them to the person with whom we disagree, we begin to understand ourselves better as well. Third, when we disagree with others and then work together to solve a problem, we may create a far better solution than we could have thought of on our own. Two minds are indeed often better than one. Fourth, this process teaches children to argue comfortably.

Just telling kids that you have confidence in their ability to work it out themselves will often work after they have been taught the techniques of problem solving. We need not feel that we have to intervene in every fight. We must leave responsibility in the hands of the children, where it belongs. Ideally, children should resolve conflicts themselves. If we have been intervening in the past, it's important to let them know that "From now on, I'm not going to get involved in your conflicts." They may not catch on right away—don't expect an instant change for any of you. There are times, especially when emotions are running high or the issue in dispute is critical to one or both children or time is of the essence, that the adult may have to intervene and assist in the problem-solving process.

Siblings are lucky to have brothers and sisters to fight with. Sibling rivalry can become an opportunity for growth if it is kept to a minimum, and then when it does occur it is used to teach children how to solve their own problems. Even when our children cannot resolve their conflicts to their liking, they learn how to cope and adjust. Sometimes their conflicts may not be easily resolved, but they can still live with the person and respect his or her rights.

A school counselor asked a kindergarten child, "What's the worst thing in the world?" The child responded, "When my sister teases me." "And what's the best thing in the world?" the counselor continued. "When my sister plays with me."

SUMMARY OF MAIN POINTS

• Sibling rivalry is a normal by-product of family life.

• We have not failed as parents if our children fight.

• Parents can eliminate or minimize some sources of sibling rivalry.

• Parents can use problem-solving techniques to figure out how to handle some sibling fights when they're involved in them.

♦ Parents can teach their children how to use problem-solving techniques to settle fights between themselves.

♦ Brothers and sisters can learn how to use problem-solving techniques to settle their own fights without their parents' help.

CHAPTER TEN

What's Fair to Expect at Each Age

Just imagine teaching young infants how to share! How can they share if they do not yet even realize that there is a world beyond themselves? Trying to teach babies to share would be quite a frustrating undertaking.

Wouldn't it also be absurd *not* to expect ten-year-olds to share? By ten, children are well aware that they are not alone in this world. If we don't expect them to share, we are remiss in our responsibility to teach them how to get along with others.

In order to successfully teach discipline to children, we must know what's fair to expect of them at each age. Ideally, children's responsibilities and freedom should increase with age. As they get older, we can expect more of them while giving them more privileges. In reality, often just the opposite happens—the older our children get, the more limits and restrictions we place on them.

Many six-year-olds are given more freedom and independence than sixteen-year-olds.

We can get caught up in discipline problems because we either expect too much of our children too soon or expect too little of them too late. Adjusting our expectations to the developmental level of our children is often a challenge. Let's explore some general characteristics of children at each age and then how discipline can be adapted to these characteristics. Please keep in mind that the ages are approximate and are just meant to give you a general frame of reference.

BABIES (BIRTH TO ABOUT ONE YEAR)

"I Want It Now!"

Newborn babies cannot wait to have their needs met. We have to pay attention to their cries, try to figure out what they need, and give it to them right away in order to help them adjust to life outside the womb.

Try to picture what it must be like for newborn babies! For nine months they sit cozy and secure inside their mother's womb, with all their physical needs being met automatically. They're never hungry or cold. They blissfully reside in a secure and predictable world of their own. Then suddenly, one day, they are pushed out into a world where nothing comes automatically—neither warmth, food, nor comfort—and they are totally dependent on others to meet all their physical needs. Learning to trust that this world is a safe place where they will have their needs met is a major challenge for every baby.

However, as the first year progresses, babies need to gradually learn how to wait to have their needs met. They can learn to tolerate a little frustration by having to wait short periods of time. For example, although when babies are first born they need their food as soon as they are hungry, by the time they are one year old, they no longer have to be fed immediately. They can wait to have their meals at set times.

Learning to wait builds trust in children—trust that others will pull through for them and trust in themselves to be able to make it through. Knowing how to wait for what we want is self-control, an important aspect of good discipline. However, babies should never have to wait so long that they lose any hope and become extremely agitated. Too much frustration teaches babies to be wary in an unpredictable world.

"Listen to Me"

Crying is the way babies talk to us. They cry to tell us they are hungry, wet, tired, too cold, or too hot. They cry to tell us when they are in pain or when they just want to be held. It's sometimes quite a challenge to figure out exactly what message they are sending. Until we do, their cries can really get on our nerves.

Not being able to stop the crying can make us feel like failures. Angry and frustrated with the baby, we may be tempted to punish or hit him to get him to stop. But if we do that, we will only make our babies cry louder, and we will hurt our relationship with them.

When you have a crying baby, try the following:

1. Check to see if the baby is hungry, messy, cold, hot, in pain, or sick. Feeding, burping, changing a diaper, putting on or taking off clothes, or calling a doctor for advice may solve the problem.

2. If not, perhaps the baby is either tired or just wants to be held. Try to rock and cuddle the baby. Babies love gentle motion and also love the security of being wrapped or held closely. Try to sing or play soft music.

3. If this doesn't work, try to put the baby to sleep. If the baby is still crying after a few minutes, try rocking again. A ride in a stroller or car may help.

4. If nothing seems to be working and you are losing your patience, which happens to most parents at one time or another, try to find someone else to take the baby for a while and give you a break. If this isn't possible, then put the baby in the crib or another safe place, and go to a different room to get yourself together. Leaving a crying baby alone in a safe place is far better than being with the baby and losing your cool.

"Pay Attention to Me"

Babies' needs are not only physical. Babies need lots of attention. They need to be hugged, cuddled, and talked to. They will not be spoiled by this attention to their needs. In fact, it will help them to become more secure and confident and thus more receptive to discipline teaching when they are older.

Taking care of babies can wear us out and tax our patience. But if we ignore them and try to get them not to be so attached to us, they'll keep bothering us more and more. Sometimes when babies begin to crawl, they will cling to our ankles, and it can be most annoying. Scolding them or pushing them away will probably only make matters worse. Getting down at their level and talking to them will probably stop their demanding behavior, at least for a while. Helping babies develop a secure attachment to us is not spoiling them. To the contrary, it is setting a foundation of security and trust that will enable them to successfully venture out into the world.

"Wow! What's All This?"

"Wow, what's all this? Where did that come from?" might pop into a baby's mind as his own hand or foot passes through his field of vision. As they flail their hands around, little by little they figure out that they are responsible for making those hands move and that the hands are connected to their body.

Once they realize that they are in control of their bodies, babies start to use them to figure out the world around them. These little explorers touch, feel, and taste anything and everything that is within their reach. Sometimes their explorations result in throwing and breaking.

As our babies start to grow, how can we encourage them without exposing them to danger and without letting them wreak havoc and destruction?

- Childproof your home by removing breakable and dangerous objects from their reach. It's too early to teach them not to touch for two reasons. First, their minds aren't developed well enough to understand why. Second, exploring the world around them develops their brains.

- Make a trade. When babies pick up something breakable, swap the object for something acceptable. Even if they fuss a bit, they will soon get distracted and involved with the new object.

- Remove them from harm. When they start to crawl, you can gently say "no" and take them away from a trouble spot.

Thus, we can set off on a positive, constructive approach to discipline. One way babies learn the trust they need to be responsive to our discipline when they are older is by having the freedom to explore their world without worrying about getting hurt, either by objects or people.

Summary

Babies cannot obey rules. The best way to teach babies discipline is to build their trust in the world and its people. You can do this by giving them attention when they need it, by keeping their world safe, and by gradually helping them learn how to wait a little for what they want. This trust they develop in the first year of life will lay the groundwork for their being able to listen to and respect our guidance as they get older.

TODDLERS (ABOUT ONE TO THREE YEARS)

"Me Do It"

Toddlers delight in the newfound freedom and independence they acquire as soon as they become upright and can get around on their own. Intoxicated by their newly acquired power, toddlers want to do for themselves. "Me do it!" are the favorite words of toddlers. We should try to let them do what they can.

However, venturing out into the world can seem quite formidable. One minute toddlers will run away from us, yelling "No!" and the next they will be running toward us wanting to be hugged and held. They come back to us for a security check and reassurance every once in a while. They're still not as independent as they think, and they still need our guidance.

When it comes to toddlers, the million-dollar discipline question is: How can we keep our sanity, protect them and our possessions from harm, and at the same time encourage their autonomy? Here are some suggestions that work:

Let them do what they can.

Decide which tasks or parts of tasks they are capable of performing for better or for worse. Be sure you are willing to accept the "for worse" results if they happen. This is easier to do if you keep in mind that when they learn to do things on their own, life will be easier for you later on.

Toddlers can feed themselves. What a mess! Usually more food ends up on the floor, the high chair, their clothes, and their hair than in their stomachs. Yes, cleaning up after them can be a pain. Try to remind yourself how this independence benefits their self-esteem and that the sooner they master the art of feeding themselves, the sooner you will not have to do it for them.

Toddlers can help dress themselves. They can bring their shoes to you even if they can't tie them. They can put on their socks. Given some options, they can choose what to wear. It certainly would be faster to put on their socks than let them do it themselves. Picking out their outfits takes far less time than allowing them to choose what they would like to wear. Letting toddlers do what they can is time-consuming in the short run, but far more parental time and energy is saved in the long run.

Toddlers can set the pace for learning to use the bathroom. This is one of the major areas where toddlers test out their autonomy. If we are anxious and try to pressure them into giving up diapers, many toddlers will resist all attempts to toilet train them just to prove that they are in charge. We start to wonder whether they'll be wearing diapers to first grade! It helps to think of this task as "toilet learning" rather than "toilet training." The focus is switched from doing something to the child to having the child do something on his own. Usually children themselves know when they are ready to learn how to use the bathroom and just need a bit of encouragement and support from us.

Child-proof.

We can set up the toddlers' world so that they are not tempted to go astray rather than constantly telling them "no" or "don't" or punishing them after they get into trouble. The road to positive discipline begins here. Putting plugs in electric sockets works far better than slapping a child's wrist for touching the outlets.

Removing breakables from the toddler's reach certainly is more effective than yelling at the child not to touch or punishing him after he breaks the object.

Distract.

"Look what I have over here" diverts many a toddler from venturing off somewhere he should not go or touching something he shouldn't. Distractions can be used to keep toddlers out of trouble.

Substitute.

"I have something here for you." Substituting an appropriate object for an inappropriate object is also an effective way to allow a toddler to learn about the world on her own without creating problems. A children's book can be a welcome substitute for a valuable encyclopedia; a toy hammering set can be an acceptable alternative to a real hammer; an interesting puzzle can replace an interesting knickknack. You can sometimes expect a few moments of fussing when the substitution is made, but soon most toddlers will get involved in the new object. If your first substitution does not work, try another.

"You Can't Make Me"

When toddlers' autonomy is threatened, they become stubborn and uncooperative. If they feel that they are being forced to do something, their backs are up against the wall. If they have no graceful way out of a situation, many toddlers will choose to stand stubbornly firm. The more insistent we are that they do things our way, the more insistent they become. When a power struggle erupts, everyone loses, both parents and children. "You can't make me" also ranks among toddlers' favorite phrases. They're often right—we really can't make them.

And we really shouldn't try to make them. It's unrealistic to expect toddlers to instantly do as we say. They need to feel that they are independent in some aspects of their lives. Here are some suggestions for avoiding power struggles yet getting our toddlers to do what they are told:

Give them a choice.

"Would you like to wear the red or the blue socks" works better than "Put on your socks now." Rather than demanding, word your request in a way that makes them feel they have some say in the matter. This allows them to maintain a sense of autonomy while you achieve their cooperation.

Save "no" for what is important.

Even with safe environments, distractions, substitutions, and choices, toddlers will still get into trouble, and there will be occasions when we have to tell toddlers no. At times, we must let them directly know that their behavior is inappropriate and gently remove them from the situation.

If toddlers go near the street, say a clear "No, you cannot go out into the street because you might get hurt," and take them away from the street. If they do it again, take them inside if you can. If a child bites others, try to notice ahead of time when this is about to happen, grab the child, and tell him "no." Try to give him alternative ways to let out his anger such as playing with a toy hammering set. If a child throws food, tell him, "No, food is for eating." Remove the food if the child persists in throwing it. (This may even be the child's way of telling you he is not hungry.)

Keep your cool.

Many toddlers have tantrums when they are upset or overtired. Sometimes this is how they let out excess energy. Other times this is how they show their frustration and disappointment. Regardless, if we keep our cool, they are less likely to keep it up. If we throw a tantrum and yell and scream because we can't stand them yelling and screaming, we're just reinforcing this technique for them, and they'll use it again and again.

If we think that we are being fair, we should try not to give in to their tantrum just because they are upset or because they are embarrassing us. Otherwise, they'll figure out that they can use tantrums to intimidate us into letting them have their way.

Summary

Some parents think that they have to be strict and punish toddlers to set them on the right course for discipline. They feel that without strict limits, toddlers will grow into wild, undisciplined children. However, just the opposite is true. Harsh demands and reprimands get toddlers' backs up and are counterproductive. Successfully disciplining toddlers means using distractions, substitutions, choices, as well as an occasional "no" to set limits in a way that will allow their autonomy to flourish. Successfully disciplining toddlers means giving them the freedom to explore this world and satisfy their curiosity while keeping them safe and protected.

PRESCHOOLERS (ABOUT THREE TO FIVE YEARS)

"Hmmm, What's This All About?"

Pouring salt in the sugar bowl and sugar in the salt shaker can seem quite fascinating to a three-year-old who's trying to figure out the nature of these substances. Painting the wall with finger paints may seem like a terrific way to decorate the room to a four-year-old. Taking apart objects to explore them and believing that they can restore them to their original condition after their experiments is a favorite activity of many preschoolers. Their job is exploring and deciphering the fascinating world around them. The major challenge for children during their preschool years is to develop the initiative to come up with ideas of their own and try them out.

These little scientists certainly pose quite a challenge for us. Cleaning up after their experiments can be a nightmare. It's awfully hard to keep your cool when you find your clock taken apart into thirty pieces or all your stamps licked and stuck to different papers. Before you react, try to take a deep breath, settle down, and say to yourself, "Curiosity is often the sign of a good student." It really is. The curiosity children develop at this stage stands them in good stead throughout their school years. Curiosity also helps children gain social acceptance because their knowledge about different topics attracts other children to them.

Certainly, we cannot let preschoolers conduct any experiment they want. Our home would be in a shambles, and they could hurt themselves. How can we help them develop their curiosity and sense of initiative while keeping them safe and out of trouble?

Remove temptations.

Just as with younger children, eliminating temptations prevents many problems from ever occurring. Removing dangerous objects from their reach (which gets higher and higher very quickly), putting childproof locks on cabinets that contain harmful products, and having them play in fenced-in areas are some of the steps we can take.

Provide interesting toys.

Toys that can be taken apart and put together provide a constructive outlet for preschoolers' drive for initiative. Legos, puzzles, blocks, and interesting objects are their tools. There's no need to buy fancy electronic toys. They often squelch children's curiosity rather than develop it.

Enforce natural/logical consequences.

What do you do if toddlers persist with an activity after you have told them to stop? Enforce natural and/or logical consequences. When a child continues to paint the wall after being given paper, say, "Painting on the wall messes it up. I will have to take away your paints."

"Why? Why? Why?"

"Why is the sky blue?" "Why do birds fly?" "Why doesn't God fall out of the sky?" "Why do dogs bark?" are typical questions preschoolers pose as they try to figure out what this world is all about. The barrage of *whys* can drive parents crazy. Many times, we don't even know the answers to these questions ourselves.

You may recall this famous story. Four-year-old Ryan asked his mom where he came from. Mom promptly went to the bookcase, took out a stack of books, and proceeded to give Ryan a detailed explanation of how babies are born. When she was through, Ryan asked, "But where did I come from before we moved here last year?" Try to find simple, direct answers to their questions.

It is often helpful to talk to them about their question before answering it. That way you can figure out whether they are indeed asking about the facts of life or just where they used to live. Telling them to be quiet, laughing at their questions, or telling them that children should be seen and not heard will only stifle their healthy curiosity. They need to ask questions in order to learn.

"I Am the Center"

As toddlers, children acquire a sense of self. As preschoolers, they learn to love this new self. They think that they are the center of the universe and that the world revolves around them. If they do not see something, it does not exist. If their eyes are closed, no one can see them.

Egocentric is an adjective often used to describe preschoolers. While it may seem that way on the surface, egocentric preschoolers are not just miniature selfish, self-centered adults who want everything their way. Egocentrism is a normal step in the development of the young child. They're supposed to act that way. Adults aren't. Preschoolers are just beginning to figure out their own needs and interests. They must accomplish that task before they can think of the needs and interests of others.

Preschoolers have a very difficult time understanding the point of view of others. How can we help them to do so?

Explain how their actions affect others.

"If you take all the toys from the baby, the baby will be bored and will cry." "If you keep all the blocks for yourself, your friends might not want to come back to play with you."

Explaining to preschoolers how they can be sensitive to the feelings of others also helps them realize that others are important as well. "Let's put the dog in the yard because Julie is afraid of him." "When you squeeze the baby too hard, it hurts the baby."

Encourage pretend play.

Activities such as pretend play help preschoolers practice getting along in this world. Playing house—taking care of the baby, going off to work, cooking meals—helps children learn how to behave and relate to people. Allowing children to dress up and act out roles helps prepare them for life as grown-ups and helps them understand other people's feelings and needs.

Explain the effects of their actions.

Tell preschoolers why they must stop their inappropriate behavior, and direct them toward something that is safe for them to explore. This approach helps them develop the understanding of the world they are seeking. "Blocks are not for throwing. They can hurt people. You can throw this Nerf ball."

Enforce natural/logical consequences.

If preschoolers persist even after your explanations and redirections, then it is time to enforce natural/logical consequences. "I will not play with you anymore now because it hurts me when you climb on my back." (See chapter 7.)

Summary

Curiosity about this world is an attribute that will stand preschoolers in good stead throughout their lives. They need time and freedom to explore their surroundings, to ask questions, to take objects apart and put them together again, and to engage in pretend play. If preschoolers are labeled "selfish" and "inconsiderate," they will probably live up to this image. If, however, their self-centeredness is instead understood and accepted as a normal part of their development, they will soon outgrow it. Disciplining preschoolers means directing and redirecting their curiosity to acceptable outlets, explaining the effects of their actions on others, and enforcing logical or natural consequences when all else fails.

SCHOOL-AGE CHILDREN (ABOUT SIX TO TWELVE YEARS)

"I Can Do It"

Reading, writing, and arithmetic are but a few of the skills that children must master once they enter school. Physical skills such as playing ball, jumping rope, and skating; academic skills such as working with computers, figuring out math and science, and reading; interpersonal skills such as cooperating and getting along with others—these are all critical accomplishments at this age. Learning that they are capable people is the primary achievement of this period. Some children have a harder time finding their strengths, particularly if academic subjects do not come easily to them. How can you help them at home to achieve this feeling of competence and success?

Spark their interest.

Try to find a topic that sparks your child's interest and through which she can experience success. Baseball cards, sports cars, dolls, chess, and stamps are among the many areas that might spark an otherwise unmotivated child's interest. By becoming an expert in one of these areas, your child can develop a feeling of competence so essential at this age. Children who feel competent tend to feel good about themselves and are less likely to act up and misbehave.

Work together to solve learning problems.

Punishing children for poor achievement in school often backfires. Many children dig in their heels and refuse to improve their work if they feel pressured to do so. Other children improve their work but then get back at their parents some other way.

School-age children want to and need to feel successful. They just may not know how to succeed. Try to work together with your child and your child's teacher to figure out strategies that will lead to your child's success. Breaking down tasks into smaller segments, working together with another classmate, making lists of assignments, and planning the times these assignments will be done are among the kinds of strategies that help solve some learning problems. See chapter 11 for a discussion of the report card issue.

"Let's Share"

As hard as it may be to admit, once our children start school, we are no longer the center of their universe. Friends and teachers start to play a vital role in shaping their lives. As they approach school age, children become ready to shift their focus from learning about themselves to learning about the needs and feelings of those around them.

School-age children need to learn to work out their differences and to cooperate with others. Before they get to school, children live in a world that more or less revolves around them and their needs. The school experience brings them into a larger, more populated world filled with people who have many needs that may conflict with theirs. How can we help our children learn social skills?

Assign chores.

If all family members have chores whereby they all pitch in and help around the house, in addition to learning how to cooperate, children will also learn responsibility.

Hold family meetings.

At scheduled times, once a week perhaps, the whole family can meet to discuss their concerns. Problems between people, family plans, and general gripes are among the topics that can be discussed. Each family member is given the opportunity to speak without being interrupted. Then the family together attempts to solve any problems and resolve any conflicts. These meetings help children learn to listen to and be sensitive to the needs of others and to develop a cooperative spirit.

Provide cooperative games.

Encourage your children to play cooperative games. Groups of children or children and adults together can play these games. The bickering and fighting that are so annoying when siblings play competitive games disappears. Cooperative games help eliminate some discipline hot spots. (See *Everyone Wins!* by S. Luvmour and J. Luvmour for more on cooperative games.)

"I Can Reason"

While younger children are so new to life that they really don't understand how all the pieces of their world fit together, school-age children have a concrete understanding of how their world works. They should be able to reason and understand the relationship between cause and effect and thus understand the effects of their actions on others. These children need to be told when and why people are angry, disappointed, or frustrated with their behavior. Expressing our feelings directly and nonhurtfully (see chapter 5) will help teach them sensitivity to others, responsibility for their own behavior, and how to express themselves constructively.

All school-age children misbehave and make mistakes as they try to figure out how this world works. Unlike with younger children, you can now use reasoning when disciplining them. Here are some suggestions for using reasoning to teach them not to misbehave while at the same time nurturing their sense of competence:

Set clear, fair limits.

School-age children are capable of understanding the reasons for rules and the effects of not obeying rules. While certainly the final decision about limits should remain in the hands of the parents, children need to express their ideas and concerns about their rules. By listening to children's views about our rules, why they are or are not fair, and by explaining our reasons when they differ from theirs, we convey the message that they are capable thinkers.

Don't try to fix all their mistakes for them.

Sometimes it's so tempting to fix everything for our children. We hate to see them disappointed or upset when their toy breaks or they have lost something. However, when they experience the result of not taking care of their own property, such as loss or breakage, children soon learn to become more responsible for their possessions. They become competent caretakers. While it is understandable that we might want to resort to anything to prevent the crying that follows a broken toy, solving our children's problems for them robs our children of the opportunity to learn responsibility for their actions.

Allow them to experience the natural/logical consequences of their misbehavior.

Our children's ability to reason concretely and to see the relationship between cause and effect is developed at this age. Therefore, they are ideally suited for an approach involving logical consequences. Not being allowed to use the ball after not putting it away, not being able to ride a bike for a week after riding it someplace forbidden, and having to earn money to replace a broken window are the kinds of consequences that teach school-age children responsibility. Making them accountable teaches them that they are competent and powerful.

Excusing their behavior conveys the message that we do not think they are capable of assuming responsibility. They learn to blame others for their problems and do not consider themselves to be accountable for their actions. This behavior, in turn, fosters a sense of incompetence.

Harsh punishments that are meant to get back at the child for misbehaving and that do not logically follow from the misbehavior also rob children of responsibility and a feeling of competence because the children lose any sense of control in the situation.

Teach them how to solve their own problems.

Their minds are now capable of learning the specific steps of problem solving in an orderly fashion. By learning how to state a problem, brainstorm solutions, select a solution, try it out, and decide whether it works, children learn to feel good about their ability to cope with life. When they first begin school, children need direct guidance in the problem-solving process. As they get older, they can learn to do the problem-solving steps on their own. As problem solving becomes second nature to them, they become more and more secure in themselves and their ability to face what life brings. See chapter 8 for details about this approach.

Teach them how to settle their own disagreements.

If we can do this, our children will develop competence and we will have fewer headaches. Isn't it infuriating when we feel that we have to constantly intervene in fights? "Quit that fighting or I'll take away the game." "If you keep on fighting, I'll send you to your rooms." "Give her the toy. She had it first and you're bigger than she is." Instead, if we teach them how to listen to each other's point of view, state the problem, and work on a compromise solution together, we have fewer headaches and they feel much better about themselves and each other. As they discuss their disagreements, their ability to understand the relationship between cause and effect develops.

Summary

As we teach our school-age children discipline, we must keep in mind their critical need at this period to feel that "I am a capable person" and "I can do things." They are indeed capable of thinking logically on a very concrete level (more abstract thinking will develop during the next stage). Teaching them discipline means teaching them the self-control they need to cooperate and get along with others and to solve their own problems. The key is *self-control*—that they are capable and competent to do things for and by themselves.

TEENAGERS
(ABOUT THIRTEEN TO EIGHTEEN YEARS)

"What's Happening to Me?"

Teenagers are brewing and bubbling chemical factories. Their hormones are raging. At no other time in their lives do people experience such dramatic changes in their bodies so quickly. Adjusting physically and emotionally to all these changes can be quite stressful.

Almost overnight, teenagers seem to be transformed from cute little children to awkward, self-conscious semiadults, semichildren. It's no wonder relating to them presents such a challenge to us parents.

"Who Am I?"

"Who am I?" "What do I believe?" "What will I become?" As our children enter the teen years and become more independent and venture farther out, they wake up to a whole new world of ideas and values. They start to take a second look at their families and try to decide for themselves who they are and what they believe. They no longer accept our ideas at face value. They argue and debate with us, challenge our every word, resist our guidance and direction—a nightmare at times for us but a normal step for them on the road to responsible adulthood.

The only way our teens can figure out who they themselves are is by breaking away from us and becoming more independent—but not totally. The teen years in some ways echo the toddler period; like toddlers, teens need to be independent and explore on their own, but at the same time they need to be able to return to us to touch base. One minute they're disowning us, the next minute they're begging us for help. How can we meet the discipline challenge that this independence brings?

Give them some leeway.

While tight pants with holes, shaved hair, multiple earrings, and other unconventional garb may embarrass or offend us, they're a pretty harmless way to let teens feel that they can be themselves and different from those they depend on. Teens need leeway. We need to loosen up on our limits and trust that they will make wise decisions. If we give them some slack in unimportant areas such as dress, then they will be more likely to obey us on issues that really matter to us. Effective discipline for teens means setting limits primarily for critical issues of health and safety, of both themselves and others. Remember, they need to try to be different from us in order to figure out who they are. Unless we carefully pick our battles with them, we will be in trouble.

Don't take their changes personally.

Teens dress and act differently from us because they need to experiment with other approaches in order to figure out who they are. Most teens go through this phase; it is not a rejection of you and your values but rather a test for themselves.

"You Can't Make Me"

Ultimatums make teens feel weak and dependent just at a time when they are struggling to become independent, separate beings. "You'd better do this or else" is a great way to get a teen to rebel. Instead of giving ultimatums, try the following:

Explain your point of view and listen to theirs.

Discuss your expectations, listen to their feelings, be willing to change when they make a good case for their point of view, and stand firm when you know you are right.

Focus on the situation rather than on them.

When setting limits, focus on concerns about the situation rather than their behavior. "I don't trust the situation with guys and girls all sleeping in one room. I trust you but I cannot trust what might happen with some of the others." "I trust that you won't be drinking, but I am concerned about what those who are drinking might do."

Give them hope.

Once your trust is violated, encourage them to earn the trust back. "When you have proved that you can keep your word, then . . ." Try to refrain from messages like "I can never trust you again." If we want kids to behave appropriately, then we have to give them hope that they can change their behavior when they mess up.

"Reason with Me"

Teens can understand what we mean when we use abstract concepts like fairness, justice, and peace. We don't have to be so concrete and specific with them when we discuss our rules and consequences as we do with younger children. "It's not fair to me to leave me anxious and worried about your safety" and "Please do this for the sake of family peace" are phrases that teens can understand.

Teens practice their newly acquired skill of abstract reasoning by questioning our ideas. "Why do you dislike him? I think he's a nice guy." "You're so old-fashioned." "You're prejudiced."

How can we discipline them when they are so argumentative?

Keep in mind that they are exercising their brains.

Try to look at their questioning of our opinions, rules, and decisions as an intellectual exercise, not as a threat to our authority. Teens argue over everything. It's a pain for us parents, but teens are supposed to argue. That's how they learn to think for themselves.

Don't give up if you know you're right.

Setting limits can be exasperating at a time when our children are testing their wings and their minds. "It's not worth the hassle." "I'll just let him do what he wants." "If he thinks he can handle everything, I'll let him." "He'll just have to suffer the consequences." What happens if we decide to give in and let teens do whatever they want because we are tired of all the arguing? They'll figure we don't care enough to set down limits. When this happens, many teens will keep pushing and pushing, getting into more and more trouble, until we finally take some action. While they may not consciously be able to express or admit this, teens consider it a sign of love and caring when their parents set reasonable limits and endure all the hassles that go along with enforcing them.

Summary

What is a successful approach to discipline for teens? One that allows them enough leeway to disagree with us and to try to be different from us while at the same time providing enough limits so that they do not venture dangerously off course. Discipline for teens means allowing age-appropriate avenues of freedom that are balanced with responsibilities.

As argumentative and rebellious as they may seem, teens need our love and nurturing. They need to know when we're proud of them, when they've made a wise decision. Try not to feel rejected as teens break away and become their own selves; it's another step on the road to adulthood.

AGES AND STAGES

MOMMY: *Becca, you have to learn to tie your shoes. You'll be going to kindergarten soon and the teacher will expect you to know how to tie your shoes.*

BECCA: *I tried Mommy, I can't do it.*

MOMMY: *Don't say "can't," Becca.*

BECCA: *But I can't; I tried it, and I can't.*

MOMMY: *You will have to learn to say "I can—I can do it," and then you will do it.*

BECCA: *But, Mommy, I can't do it! See, I try, but I can't do it.*

MOMMY: *Remember the story of the Little Engine That Could? He kept saying, "I think I can, I think I can," and he did it.*

"I think I can, I think I can" are not magic words. We can't always do what we think we can. Yes, we should have a positive outlook, but realism is also important.

Just because a child reaches a certain age does not mean his behavior will totally conform to the general age and stage descriptions provided in this chapter. Ages and stages are only one clue to our children's behavior. Family dynamics, the relationship between parents, and the child's position in the family all play a role in a child's development. Children are born with different temperaments—some are calm, some active, some quiet, some shy, some boisterous. Their personal temperament helps determine the course of their development. Their natural talents and abilities also play a role in how they blossom. We must also not forget that events that occur in their lives, particularly if they are traumatic, have a developmental impact. Our approach to discipline must take all this into account.

DEVELOPING A SENSE OF RESPONSIBILITY AS CHILDREN GROW

Being a parent sure is an all-consuming job—so many responsibilities and decisions that directly affect the life of another human being. It seems overwhelming at times. But why make it harder on ourselves than it needs to be? We can shift some of those decisions and responsibilities to our children. We'll all be better off. Let's look at what happened one morning between Mom and her son Jeff, nine years old:

MOM: *Jeffrey, Jeffrey.*

JEFF: (voice from the bedroom) *What do you want, Mom?*

MOM: *Get up, it's time for school.*

JEFF: *Not yet, Mom, it's still early.*

MOM: *It's already 7:30, Jeff, you had better get up.*

JEFF: *Okay, okay.*

MOM: *Jeff, are you up?*

JEFF: *Yeah, I'm up, Mom, what should I wear?*

MOM: *Why don't you wear your jeans and your blue striped shirt?*

JEFF: *What socks?*

MOM: *Your blue ones. Hurry, your breakfast is on the table.*

JEFF: *By the way, Mom, my teacher wants picture money. Yesterday was the last day, and I forgot to bring it. So remind me, will you, Mom?*

MOM: *Yes, but I'm afraid you may lose it on your way to school. So why don't I bring it to school for you. I'll leave it in the office with your name on it.*

JEFF: *That's okay with me. Oh, on your way to school, will you drop off my library books? They're already overdue.*

MOM: *Sure.*

Picture yourself rushing around, trying to get yourself and your family off for the day, and you have to keep checking back with your child to make sure he's up. Don't you have enough on your mind already? Certainly, at nine years old, Jeff could set his own alarm and wake up on time for school. You don't need this extra hassle. Jeff doesn't need it, either. Jeff needs to learn to do things for himself.

Why is Mom doing everything for Jeff? She may mean well, figuring that he's just a child and needs extra help. Or she may feel a need to be the one in charge. Or perhaps she needs to have someone depend on her.

Responsibility and Independence

Mom may think that her approach is the easy way out, but not only is she making it harder on herself, she is making it harder on Jeff as well. What messages does Jeff get when his mother waits on him hand and foot—that he is incapable of taking care of his own needs, that he does not know how to make good decisions, that he is too weak to assume responsibility for his own mistakes, and that he doesn't need to assume responsibility because someone will always be there to pick up after him. What will happen to this little boy's self-esteem? What will happen to him in school when he's given assignments and responsibilities and there's one teacher for twenty-five children? How will he learn to develop self-discipline? How will he be able to survive in this world on his own? Won't he resent his mother when he is older?

Children gradually need to learn to assume responsibility for themselves while they're under their parents' tutelage. Otherwise, when they set foot into the world on their own, they will be lost, overwhelmed by the multitude of responsibilities that independence brings. One of the most important parts of discipline is to teach kids responsibility and self-discipline so they can make it in the world on their own.

A golden rule of parenting is NEVER DO FOR A CHILD WHAT A CHILD CAN DO FOR HIM/HERSELF. As soon as our children are physically and emotionally ready to take on new responsibilities, we should allow them to. It's good for everyone. However, two problems sometimes get in the way of this happening:

Problem 1.

Kids develop so gradually that we may fail to notice when a child is ready for new responsibilities. How can we help ourselves figure out when our children are ready for new responsibilities?

Solutions.

Observe what is expected of them in school. Are we expecting fewer responsibilities than they can handle at school? Does the teacher require them to keep track of their belongings while we don't? Does the teacher expect them to budget their own time?

Reevaluate your expectations at each major transition in your child's life—going from crawling to walking, diapers to underpants, home or childcare to pre-school, pre-school to kindergarten, kindergarten to first grade, first grade to second grade, day camp to overnight camp, and on and on. Each change often marks the ability to take on new responsibilities (and privileges as well, of course). See the first part of this chapter for developmental guidelines.

Observe other children your child's age and talk to other parents. But beware: Each child is different and has different needs. For example, one child may be able to tell time in first grade while her classmate may not tell time but can tie his shoes. One may be able to set an alarm, while his friend cannot do this but can work with a computer. Children master skills at different rates and at different times.

Watch out for parents who expect too much too soon of their children, and don't let them convince you that your child's normal behavior is immature. Often these are the parents who brag about how much their children can do. Use your common sense. Just because someone else makes their five-year-old child clean all the toilets does not mean that you have to! When parents expect too much too soon of their children, often their children feel hopeless, like they can never live up to their parents' expectations. "I can't do it; I'm no good."

Engage in some personal reflection. Sometimes the first sign that we think our kids could do more to help out is our resentment. If you seem to be getting annoyed frequently and feeling like a martyr because so much responsibility falls onto you, then try to figure out how your children can pitch in and help you out. Here are some suggestions of the kinds of responsibilities children can assume at different ages:

Eating:

Toddlers: feed themselves with their hands and then eventually with silverware.

Preschoolers: help make sandwiches, puddings, cookies, and other food.

Early grades: make sandwiches, cold food, salads.

Later elementary: cook simple foods, such as eggs, toast, salads, hamburgers.

Teens: prepare whole meals.

Household chores:

Toddlers: put away toys with assistance, hold dustpan, put clothes in the hamper, sweep with carpet/floor sweeper. (Make hay while the sun shines—toddlers love to imitate us dusting, washing counters . . .)

Preschoolers: dust, pick up trash in yard, sort laundry, carry laundry, put clothes in drawers, remove plates from table and place in sink, set table.

Early grades: make their bed, hang up clothes, set table, clear dishes from table, rinse dishes, feed animals, walk animals.

Later elementary: vacuum, wash and dry dishes, rake yard, read to siblings, fold laundry and put away.

Teens: do laundry, iron, yardwork, run errands, baby-sit.

Problem 2.

We may not want to let go of our little children. We may want them to still be dependent on us.

Solution.

Find a way to let go. Sometimes it is indeed hard to let go, but let go we must for our own sake as well as for the sake of our children. It helps some parents to find another outlet for their energy. Volunteering in a school, a senior citizen home, a homeless shelter, or a hospital may be a very rewarding way to help yourself, your child, and others at the same time. An added bonus is that you are modeling for your child the importance of reaching out and helping those in need.

Responsibility and Cooperation

Sometimes it may seem easier to do something ourselves rather than let our children do it inefficiently or incorrectly. Picture this scene:

Mom is washing the dishes. Six-year-old Shauna picks up the broom and starts to sweep the floor. Mom takes away the broom and says:

MOM: *I'll sweep the floor myself.*
SHAUNA: *Mom, why can't I sweep it? I love to sweep.*
MOM: *You're not big enough to do a good job.*

SHAUNA: *I am, Mom. Let me try. I'll show you how good I sweep.*

MOM: *No, Shauna, you take too long. I can do it a lot faster myself.*

What message did Shauna get from Mom? "I'm not capable." "I'm a bother." "Mom doesn't like me anymore." "Next time I shouldn't bother asking."

Yes, Mom could have swept the floor faster and better than Shauna. Shauna probably wouldn't make the bed as neatly as Mom would, either—all sorts of interesting lumps may protrude. No, Shauna probably wouldn't be as thorough if she dusted the furniture. But what's more important? A picture-perfect house or a cooperative child? Children can learn how to do it our way, but the only way they will learn is if we give them the opportunity to do so. Life will be a lot easier down the road if, imperfect as it may be at first, their help is requested and appreciated.

Responsibility and Decision Making

Another way children learn responsibility is by making decisions—not all, but some of the decisions that affect them. Which decisions can they make? Decisions that will not endanger anyone's health and safety. Decisions where the benefits of the experience of making the decision outweigh the deficits caused by a poor decision.

Benefits vs. Deficits

In this chapter's first scenario, at nine years old, Jeffrey surely could have decided on his own what to wear. If he didn't know what would match, he could ask for advice. And it wouldn't be very serious if his outfit didn't match.

How about a common situation where Mom buys a birthday present for her child's friend:

MOM: *Catherine, while you were in school, I went shopping and found the nicest gift for you to give Lisa for her birthday.*

CATHERINE: *What is it, Mom?*

MOM: *Oh, you'll love it. It's the cutest little flower pin.*

CATHERINE: *Ugh, it's gross.*

MOM: (shocked) *What?*

CATHERINE: *It's awful, Mom. She won't like it. She won't.*

MOM: *Why? I think it's beautiful, Catherine.*

CATHERINE: *Well, I don't, and I'm not going to give it to her.*

MOM: *What's wrong with it?*

CATHERINE: *It's just not her type.*

MOM: *Well, I think it is.*

CATHERINE: *Well, I don't. Besides, she's my friend, not yours.*

All of us parents know how dreadfully exhausting shopping trips with children can be! It was probably a lot easier for Mom just to pick something up than to take Catherine shopping. Maybe Mom didn't trust Catherine to pick something appropriate.

But just think how important it would have been for Catherine to choose the present. She would have to take her friend's likes into account and in the process learn how to take someone else's perspective. She would be the one accountable if the friend did not like the present. She'd have to learn to live with her mistake. She would have to figure out what to buy that's within her budget.

How can you decide which decisions are appropriate for your child to make? Try to allow those that are consistent with your child's level of ability and understanding and that won't interfere with the child's safety.

Toddlers: They need guidance—give them a choice between acceptable options the adult has provided. "Do you want to wear the green shirt or the yellow shirt?" "Do you want an apple or a banana for dessert?" "Which of these toys would you like to play with?"

Preschoolers: They still need adult guidance but can be given more choices. "Which of these stories would you like to hear before going to bed?" "Would you like eggs or cereal for breakfast?" "What outfit would you like to wear?"

Elementary school: Set rough guidelines rather than giving them choices. "What would you like for breakfast? Remember, it must be healthy." "What would you like to wear today? Remember, it's hot outside." "Which clothes would you like to buy? Remember, the budget is . . ."

Teens: Set ultimate limits against offensiveness and immorality. Each family must determine its own moral standards. Try to figure out those values that are truly important to you. Choosing clothing and deciding how to decorate their bedrooms are decisions teens can make but with the knowledge that their parents reserve the right to veto offensive, dangerous, or immoral choices.

If children are not allowed to make decisions when they are little, how can they possibly know what to do as teens when they are faced with critical decisions? The younger years provide the opportunity to learn responsible decision making under adult supervision. It's best for them to make and deal with mistakes while they are still under our protective custody. This lays a solid foundation for the teen years, when we parents are often not around while critical decisions are being made—decisions about driving, drugs, alcohol, and sex. Teens who have had practice making decisions and experiencing the consequences of their mistakes when they were younger are usually more responsible, capable decision makers and feel better about themselves.

Before you've decided to allow your child to make a decision, be sure you mean it. Look at the bind this dad found himself in:

DAD: *Don't you think it's time to have your room painted, Nadia?*

NADIA: *Yes, yes, Daddy. That's a great idea.*

DAD: *What color would you like, Nadia?*

NADIA: *Pink. I love pink. It's my favorite color.*

DAD: (disappointed) *Oh, no, not pink. That's a baby color. How about white or green or even lavender?*

NADIA: *But I like pink, Daddy.*

DAD: *But I don't. That's the one color your mother and I don't like. Anything but pink.*

NADIA: *But it's my room, Daddy.*

DAD: *I realize that, but you'll get tired of pink, you'll see.*

NADIA: *No, I won't.*

DAD: *Let's drop the subject tonight. Tomorrow you may change your mind.*

NADIA: *I know I'll still want pink.*

DAD: *That's enough for tonight. Off to bed now. Good night.*

Imagine how Nadia felt having her decision overruled. Imagine how Dad felt getting himself into this bind! Many a battle between parent and child can be prevented by parents thinking the situation through before offering their children a decision-making option. "You don't really want that, do you?" or "Are you sure?" or "That's ugly" undermine children's self-confidence and their trust in our word. The moral is: If you tell your children they can decide, stick by their decision unless health or safety is a problem, or the decision will have a devastating effect for the child.

TOO MUCH RESPONSIBILITY

A whole different category of discipline problems can crop up if we expect our children to assume too much responsibility too soon—if we expect our two-year-olds to get totally dressed on their own or if we expect our preschoolers to have perfect manners or if we expect older siblings to have sole responsibility for their younger brothers and sisters or if we expect our teenagers to do all the cooking and cleaning.

Sometimes when children are given too much responsibility, they think they can handle anything—and I mean ANYTHING! Young children may try to use dangerous household equipment. Older children may think they know how much they can drink and still not be drunk. Too much responsibility gives children an inflated sense of their independence and power. This can get them into serious trouble if they then make decisions they are not yet ready to make.

Other times children may rebel and become major discipline problems when they are given too much responsibility. They may deliberately mess up a chore you have given them. They may even go out of their way to get back at you, such as by getting into trouble and embarrassing you in public.

If, after reading this chapter, you are still not sure of what's fair to expect at different ages, ask your pediatrician or a few friends. Expecting too much too soon of our children triggers discipline problems that can be remedied.

SELECTIVE RESPONSIBILITY

Vanessa was a top student and leader in her high school. Her teachers were impressed with her sense of responsibility. When Vanessa was given a task, they knew it would be done—well and on time. Her peers also looked up to her as a responsible role model.

One weekend when Vanessa's family went on a trip, their house was broken into. As soon as they discovered the break-in, they called the police. An investigator arrived and walked around the house, inspecting each room. When he came to Vanessa's room, he was appalled. "What a horrible mess the burglars made! Everything is in a shambles." Vanessa then sheepishly admitted that there was no indication that the intruders had even entered her room—that was the room's usual state.

Kids can be selectively responsible. A child may act responsibly with and toward other people but not be so responsible with chores and possessions. We can't expect perfection. Try to keep in sight what's really important in life.

COMMUNITY SERVICE: AN AVENUE TO RESPONSIBILITY

Nothing teaches responsibility better than real-life experiences. Community service is an excellent avenue for teaching children responsibility. Volunteering at a homeless shelter, tutoring a younger child, making cookies and visiting shut-ins, and cleaning up the highway are just a few of the myriad opportunities available for engaging in community service. The joy of knowing we make a difference can inspire us to do more acts of loving-kindness for others. And if we parents volunteer along with our children, so much the better. As parents, it is important for us to model responsibility—in our homes, our jobs, and our communities.

SUMMARY OF MAIN POINTS

- Teaching discipline means knowing what's fair to expect of children at each age.

- Ages and stages are one of several clues to a child's behavior.

• The best way to teach babies discipline is to build their trust in the world and its people.

• Teaching toddlers discipline means using distractions, substitutions, and choices as well as an occasional "no" to set limits while allowing their autonomy.

• Teaching preschoolers discipline means directing and redirecting their curiosity to acceptable outlets, explaining the effects of their actions on others, and enforcing natural/logical consequences when all else fails.

• Teaching school-age children discipline means teaching them self-control by setting limits, enforcing natural/logical consequences, and teaching them how to solve their own problems.

• Teaching teens discipline means allowing them appropriate avenues of freedom that are balanced with responsibilities.

• Never do for a child what a child can do for him/herself.

• As children develop, we need to adjust their responsibilities.

• Dependent children can make us feel needed. But their dependency can make them feel helpless.

• Encouraging children to help out even if it is less efficient for us helps children develop a sense of responsibility.

• Starting at a young age, children should be allowed to make some decisions in cases where their health and safety will not be endangered.

• Try to weigh the benefits of making a decision against the problems caused by allowing the child to make this decision. Ask yourself, "What benefits will my child get from making this decision?" and "Will any harm come from a poor decision in this case?"

CHAPTER ELEVEN

Common Discipline Problems

Some discipline situations are particularly challenging to us parents. In this chapter we will address the following issues that come up ever so frequently in parent workshops: How can we make mealtimes more pleasant? How can we get our children to bed on time? How should we handle allowances? How can we put a stop to our children's annoying behaviors—sassiness, lying, whining, throwing tantrums, and tattling? How can we get out of the business of nagging? How can we prevent homework and report-card battles? Keep in mind the problem-solving format (see chapter 8) as we tackle each of these issues.

MEALTIMES

Does this scene look at all familiar?

MOM: *Kids, dinner's ready.*

DREW: *I'll be there in a few minutes, I'm in the middle of
   something.*

MOM: *Kids, come right now. Dinner is getting cold.*

LEIGH: *What are we having?*

MOM: *Lasagna.*

DREW: *Yuk. I hate lasagna.*

MOM: *I worked hard making this. You'll eat it.*

LEIGH: *I love it. It's my favorite Italian food.*

At the Table

MOM: *Drew, please stop tipping your chair back.*

DREW: *Why? It's comfortable.*

MOM: *Leigh, use your napkin, please. So how was your day?
   Leigh, I said use your napkin not your shirt.*

DREW: *I'm not hungry.*

MOM: *So don't eat if you don't want to.*

Mealtime can be indigestion time in many households. Mealtime problems tend to revolve around three main issues: when children eat, what they eat, and how they behave when they're eating.

When They Eat

"I'm not hungry now." "It's too soon to eat." "I'll eat later."

These comments can frustrate any parent who has worked hard to prepare a nice meal. Not only will the food be less appetizing later, but it means that the kitchen becomes an all-night diner and you feel like a perpetual cook and dishwasher. Having set times for meals helps avoid the "I'll eat when I feel like it" response.

Do you remember back to when you were a child in school and you ate at a set time every day? Do you remember your stomach beginning to gurgle as the clock rolled around to that time on the weekend? You automatically felt hungry because you were used to eating at that time every day. So, too, if we have set mealtimes, our children will be more likely to be hungry at those times. Their bodies will be conditioned to being hungry at mealtime.

Children feel more secure when they know what is expected of them, and they are more likely to cooperate with us. Having established mealtimes is a clear expression of our expectations. Also, giving a few minutes' warning before mealtime helps children prepare themselves and make the transition from what they are doing to eating. "Kids, we have five more minutes before it's time to wash up for dinner." (Mentioning washing up for dinner this way makes it an automatic part of coming to dinner and can eliminate some of the washing-up debates. It's a given.)

What They Eat

Like adults, children have their likes and dislikes with respect to food, but their tastes are far more fickle than ours. "What, you can't stand macaroni? That used to be your favorite dish." It's a bittersweet experience for us when the six-year-old who wouldn't go near anything that even resembled a vegetable becomes a vegetarian at age sixteen.

Studies have shown that when given a choice among healthy foods, children will eat a balanced diet on their own. Children do not need a perfectly nutritionally balanced meal at every sitting. While they may not like the particular vegetable or protein that you have placed before them at that meal, perhaps there is a substitution that will have equal nutritional value and that will appeal to them, that you can provide at another meal. Relax, provide healthy options in an appetizing fashion, and with luck, eventually they will include all the nutrients they need in their diet. Just try to keep the food as attractive as possible.

Children's appetites may vary from meal to meal and day to day. For us adults, dinner is usually our biggest meal. However, not everyone's body functions that way. For some children, breakfast or lunchtime may be when they feel like eating the most.

Children should be encouraged to try new foods, but they should not be forced to do so. Negative experiences with food can leave a long-lasting impression. I still remember being forced to eat macaroni and cheese when I was at overnight camp. It took twenty years before I would even look at macaroni and cheese again. If kids are forced to eat something they can't stand, not only will they be angry at you but they will probably eliminate that very food from their diets for a good long time (which is just the opposite of our intention). Keep in mind that children's taste buds are different from those of adults and are far more sensitive.

Many parents find it helpful to start out with small portions of food. That way the food does not seem overwhelming to children and finishing it becomes a realistic goal. In addition, leaving it up to children to ask for seconds gives them a sense of self-control. Remember, children can function very well on small quantities of food. In fact, physicians are now stressing that we all would function far better if we significantly reduced our own intake of food.

Not allowing children to have dessert unless they finish everything on their plates is a risky venture. Children may become resentful. They may sneak dessert later. They may develop eating problems. They may crave sweets. Besides, if dessert is healthy, which it should be with rare exceptions, then don't we want them to eat it regardless of what else they have had for supper?

Allowing children to help plan menus and to cook some of the meals makes it more likely that they will eat what is served. Children usually will be more cooperative at mealtime if they feel they have some control over what is served. Choosing the menu and cooking the meal can be rotated among members of the family. Monday night Mom plans and cooks, Tuesday, Sister, Wednesday, Dad, Thursday, Brother, and so on.

How They Behave

Just the mention of dinnertime can make some parents' stomachs churn! They conjure up visions of children rocking on their chairs like gymnasts, shoveling food into their mouths with their hands, wiggling and squirming all over the place. Conducting a civilized conversation seems virtually impossible.

Imagine how it must feel for young children to sit at the table. Their feet don't touch the floor, adults want to talk about boring topics, and they're expected to sit still for long periods of time. Pure torture for some! So what do they do? Sit there like a potted plant and just stomach it? Hardly. They may kick their sister under the table, poke each other, wiggle, bang their silverware against their plates—you name it, some child has probably done it. What can we do to help out both us and our children?

- If it's possible, adjust their chairs so that they are comfortable. Perhaps sitting on an adjustable stool would work.

- Don't expect them to sit too long. Give them an excuse for getting up, such as taking the dishes away or getting the salt and pepper or some article of food you might need. Letting them excuse themselves from the table when they are finished makes much more sense than forcing them to wait until everyone is through eating. While leaving the table early may not be polite for adults, it may be a necessity for children. Adults enjoy lingering over their food, savoring it and the conversation as well. Not so for children. They want to get meals over with as soon as possible. They have other, more important things to do.

- Try to include children in the conversation. This may be a challenge if your children's ages cover a wide span. Calendars that have the joke of the day or the fact of the day can help focus the conversation so that all enjoy it. Most children enjoy riddles as long as they can understand them. Or perhaps you can discuss a current event that may be of interest to all. Try to keep the conversation as relaxed as possible and avoid discussions of problems such as poor schoolwork.

◆ Model good table manners. The best way to teach children good manners is to have them ourselves. Our children will learn how to eat from watching us eat. We may have to explain how to hold the fork or place a napkin in one's lap, but eventually our children will do as we do. We cannot expect young children to master the eye-hand coordination required by table manners. Their bodies and minds are not yet ready for this task.

BEDTIME

Bedtime can cause many discipline headaches. Nancy came down from her bedroom into the living room:

MOM: *Nancy, get back into bed.*
NANCY: *Not yet, Mom, I want to play awhile.*
MOM: *You played all day, Nancy. It's bedtime now.*
NANCY: *But I'm not sleepy. Besides, I'm thirsty. I want a drink.*
MOM: *Here's some water, Nancy. Now get back into bed quickly.*
NANCY: (calling down from upstairs) *M-O-T-H-E-R, something hurts me here from inside my pajamas. Please come and see what it is.*
MOM: *I'm sure there's nothing there, Nancy. You're just making up excuses. If you keep this up I won't allow you to watch your favorite television program tomorrow.*
NANCY: *I don't care about TV, Mother. I'm just not going to bed. I am going to stay up late, just like you do.*

MOM: *Oh, no, you're not, young lady.*
NANCY: *Oh, yes, I am!*

"No, I don't want to go to bed." "I'm not tired." "Read me one more story." "I'm very thirsty. I need a glass of water." "I have to go to the bathroom!" Parents can dread bedtime as much as their kids. It can seem to drag on forever, wearing down our nerves, sapping us of any energy we hoped to have left after the children have gone to bed.

Why can bedtime be such a problem? The transition between being awake and being asleep is often difficult for children to make. Going to bed means being alone. It means separating from their parents and from all the excitement of the world around them. Children often use every tactic they can to try to delay this separation.

Also, often when children lie alone in their beds in the dark, they think about all their worries and concerns. They may rehash unpleasant events that happened to them during the day. Being alone in the dark can be unsettling for them.

How can we ease the transition to sleep? Here are some suggestions for easing this transition so going to bed will become a less painful process for both parents and children:

♦ Decide a proper bedtime for your child. Remember to adjust this bedtime as your child gets older. As children get older, they should go to bed later. (Older children should have later bedtimes than their younger siblings. Even staying up ten minutes later will make them feel important.) One way to tell when it is time to adjust a child's bedtime to a later hour is if the child is unable to fall asleep for a long time for several nights in a row. Eliminating the daytime nap may also solve the problem of a young child going to bed but being unable to sleep.

• Discuss bedtime rules and times during the day, during a calm time.

• Try to keep the mood as calm as possible before bedtime. It's unreasonable to expect that a child who has just wrestled with his father or who has been watching an exciting movie or television show can suddenly settle down and get into bed. The less stimulation before sleep, the better.

• Notify your child when bedtime is approaching. "In ten minutes it will be time to brush your teeth and get ready for bed."

• Establish routines for bedtimes. When children have an established pattern of going-to-bed activities, it gives them a sense of security that makes the whole separation process seem less formidable. As we discussed previously (see chapter 3), limits help a child feel safe. "After you brush your teeth, I'll read you a story." Reading a story, telling a story, or playing music are all ways parents can help their children go to bed peacefully. You don't necessarily need a new book every night. Using the same story repeatedly can be reassuring to children.

• Keep the television off in the house until they fall asleep. Half hearing a television show can be very distracting, annoying, and sometimes upsetting. Lying in bed, children often imagine the endings to scary shows being even worse than they are.

Delaying Tactics

You read a book, chat for a few minutes, and then just as you tuck in your child and kiss him good night, he says, "By the way, Mom, I need to tell you about something that happened in school today," or "I have something important on my mind I have to talk to you about." Our children know that we do not want them to worry when they go to sleep, so they know that we will stay and talk about whatever their concern is. Sometimes, not always, children manipulate us so they can get to stay up later. But this can grate on our nerves. We need some time for ourselves. How can we eliminate delaying strategies?

* You can let them know in a nice way. "I'll be happy to talk with you tomorrow. Right now it is bedtime. I have work I must do now."

* Allow your child to read a book until he falls asleep. This will help him learn how to go to sleep on his own, and it will also save you the tension of being called back several times. Bedtime does not necessarily mean sleep time. They may stay up very late the first few times, but eventually, they will catch up on their sleep.

* Stay calm when they get out of bed, but be firm. Let them know directly that you need to have time for yourself and steer them right back to bed.

* If your child is terrified of being alone, try to gradually wean yourself away from his room. At first perhaps sit in a chair in the room. Then be in the room next door or out in the hall. Try to make a little noise so that your child knows you are still there. As you gradually increase your distance from the room, he will get used to being alone.

ALLOWANCE

Allowances can be the source of some discipline problems, but they can also lead to effective discipline teaching.

Mother is mixing a cake when seven-year-old Chad runs into the kitchen.

CHAD: *Mom, quick, give me a dollar.*

MOM: *Give you a dollar? For what?*

CHAD: *I've got to have one right away. Mitch is going down to the store to get a new yo-yo, and I want one, too. Quick! Quick! He'll go without me.*

MOM: *So let him go.*

CHAD: *But I want to go with him so I can get a yo-yo just like his. Please, Mom, give me the dollar right away.*

MOM: *But I gave you money yesterday to buy those baseball cards.*

CHAD: *Gosh, that was yesterday.*

MOM: *Chad, will this go on forever? Do you think money grows on trees?*

CHAD: *Don't be a meanie, Mom. Give me the dollar, just this once. I won't ask for anything tomorrow or the day after tomorrow. I promise, Mom. Pleeeeaaaase.*

MOM: *Okay. Give me my purse.*

Imagine how Mom must have felt! She was put on the spot and felt pressured. It's hard for many parents to turn down a request like that. They don't want to disappoint their child, and after all, he's not asking for a large amount of money. And the nagging—who can stand it? Isn't it worth a dollar just to shut off the nagging? Giving the money seems like the easy way out.

Imagine how Chad felt. He really wanted that yo-yo but had to rely on begging his mom for it, and time was of the essence. They both would have been better off if Chad had an allowance. Mom would not have been constantly harassed by requests for money, and Chad would have learned how to handle money responsibly.

An allowance is an excellent tool for setting clear monetary limits with children and for teaching children self-control as well as for teaching them the value of money. Here are some suggestions for allowances:

• Discuss it with the child and decide how much is reasonable for the child to receive at that age. Take into consideration what you feel you can afford. Be sure to adjust the allowance up as children get older. Many parents raise allowances on birthdays.

• Decide what expenses will be covered by allowance—snacks, toys, activities such as movies, school supplies, clothes (for older children), etc.

• Stick to the allowance. When a child runs out of money before the next allowance period, allow him to experience the natural consequence—he will have to wait before he spends any money. Making up excuses to supplement their allowance when they run out will only teach children that they do not have to have self-control. If they're running short of money, perhaps they can do odd jobs for you that you might have had to pay someone else to do.

• If a child keeps overspending his allowance, then problem solving (see chapter 8) together would be helpful.

• Do not use money as a punishment. "If you don't clean up your room, I will take away your allowance." This approach leads to children equating behavior with money. Then they think money can buy good or bad behavior.

Let's rewrite the scenario between Chad and his mother, this time having Chad on an allowance:

CHAD: *Mom, quick, give me a dollar.*
MOM: *Give you a dollar, Chad? What for?*
CHAD: *I've got to have one right away. Mitch is going down to the store to get a new yo-yo, and I want one, too. Quick! Quick! He'll go without me.*
MOM: *So let him go.*

CHAD: *But I want to go with him so I can get a yo-yo just like his. Please, Mom, give me a dollar right away.*

MOM: *You have an allowance. If that's what you'd like to buy, then go buy it.*

CHAD: *But I spent my allowance on baseball cards.*

MOM: *I'm sorry. I guess you'll just have to wait until next week.*

The key is not to give in to nagging. Once your child sees that you're going to stick by your policy, he'll stop nagging. If Chad had been overspending his allowance regularly, then Mom could have said the following:

MOM: *Chad, I've noticed that you've been running out of money every week for the last month. Let's see if we can figure out how to help you live within your budget.*

Then together Mom and Chad could brainstorm ideas for helping him live within his budget. Among their suggestions might be for him to divide his allowance into two sections, one for immediate spending and one for long-term saving; make a list of weekly expenses; set aside a certain amount of money for emergency purchases; wait a day to think about a purchase before buying it.

Allowances are a marvelous tool for children to experience the natural consequences of their actions, to solve problems, and to learn self-discipline.

HOMEWORK

Homework is often the source of much strife—battles between parents and children over homework are not uncommon. Let's look at how we can eliminate some of the family stress and discipline problems caused by homework by examining when and where homework is done as well as our role in the homework.

Allow Time for a Break

Give your children a break before starting their homework. Imagine what it must be like for children to sit all day long in a classroom, sometimes forbidden from getting up or speaking for a couple of hours at a time. Many children cannot even go to the bathroom when they need to but must wait for official "bathroom breaks." I spend many hours in classrooms observing my student teachers, and it has made me acutely aware of how children usually have precious little freedom of movement. So when they come home from school, they need a break. They need to have a snack, relax for a while, and just vegetate. Having them settle down immediately to do their homework may seem efficient but actually is probably just the opposite. Their minds will work better if they have had time to regenerate.

Set Aside a Special Time for Homework

Whether homework is done before supper or after supper is an individual family decision. Some parents prefer to save the homework until after supper so that they can be around to serve as a resource to their children. Other parents prefer to have their children do their homework in the afternoon, perhaps under the supervision of a baby-sitter or child-care worker in the case of younger children. Whatever the choice, what is important is that children know that there is a certain time set aside for homework. Ten o'clock at night is not the time to ask children if they have homework.

Keep the Television Off

"I'll finish my homework in time to watch my favorite TV show." Television provides an incentive for children to speed through their homework. Accuracy and thought are often compromised in the process. Many parents find it helpful to eliminate any television watching on school nights with perhaps a few exceptions for very special programs. If children know that once their homework is done, their next activity will not be dependent on a specific schedule the way TV is, they will be more likely to spend adequate time on the homework rather than rush through it. Reading, studying, playing a game, or working on a project can replace television on weekday evenings.

Problem Solve with Children Who Dawdle Through Homework.

Some children have just the opposite time problem of those who rush through their work to watch television. Rather than race through their work, they dawdle over it, taking hours to complete the simplest assignment. Some children do this because they want everything to be just perfect. Others really don't understand the work. Some feel overwhelmed and don't know where and how to begin. You may find other possible reasons for this behavior.

One helpful approach is to set a timer for however long you and your child's teacher consider to be reasonable for working on the assignment. When the timer goes off, the child can stop working. Or perhaps the teacher needs to adjust assignments. Here, once again, problem solving (see chapter 8) is a terrific tool. You, your child, and the teacher could meet. "We have a problem. It's taking Emily three hours to complete her assignments. What can we do to solve this problem?" Together, all three of you could brainstorm. Among the suggestions might be that the teacher reduce the amount of homework, Emily would do just a little bit more each evening until she works up to a full load, or that Emily gets tutoring so that she'll understand the material better. The solution to Emily's problem will be tailored to Emily, but the process of finding a solution will work for any child. Involving the child in finding a solution to the problem is essential. The child then has ownership of the solution and will be more likely to carry it out. After all, homework is the child's responsibility.

Problem Solve with Children Who Consistently Forget That They Have Homework

Some children claim they don't have homework when they really do. Working together to solve the problem is very effective in situations such as these. The homework problem gets solved, and parents and children stop fighting. Here's how it goes. After stating that the problem is "How can I remember to do my homework," the next step might be to try to brainstorm the reason why the homework is being forgotten. Perhaps it is because the child does not hear the assignment, or he doesn't know how to do it. Perhaps he has no place to write the assignment down, he's forgetful, or he just doesn't care. After these possibilities are brainstormed, then you can help the child pick the reason/s that apply to him. The next step would be to brainstorm solutions to the problem, based on the reason he chose. For example, if he realized that the problem is that he just forgets by the time he comes home, some possible solutions might be for him to have a special notebook he routinely checks each night, to tie a string to his finger to remind him, or to pin a note onto his book bag. The best solution will be the one the child selects with your guidance. That way the child is assuming responsibility for the solution and is developing self-discipline in the process.

Set Aside a Place for Homework

Every year it seems I received a notice from at least one of my children's schools telling us parents that we need to set aside a special quiet place for our children to study: a cleared desk away from any noise and with excellent lighting. What if we have no such place? Not only is this unrealistic, but I don't think it's even appropriate.

I have three children. Fortunately, all of them have usually been conscientious about doing their homework (sometimes not until the wee hours of the morning as they got older, but they did get it done). One likes to go to her room, close the door, and not be disturbed. The other two like to do their work in Grand Central Station. They need to be near people and all the hubbub in the house in order to complete their work. Often they cannot concentrate if they go off to their rooms by themselves.

One way's not right and the other wrong. It's a difference in style. Helping our children find their own styles, how and where they study best, will enhance their ability to successfully complete their homework and be self-controlled people. However, being around other people should not mean watching television. Televisions should be off when children are studying.

Establish Our Role in Homework

As parents, we can set a mood in the house that is conducive to homework being done:

♦ Keeping things calm for our children helps their minds be clear for studying and not cluttered by negative emotions. Yelling at children to do their homework sends them off in an anxious mood.

♦ Offering them a snack or a drink after they have been working a while shows them that you care.

♦ Reading or studying while they are studying sets a good example for them and establishes a studying mind-set throughout the house.

♦ Serving as a resource to them if they don't understand something enables us to help them without doing their work for them. Standing over our children monitoring their homework can convey the message that we don't have faith in them, that we think they cannot and will not do it on their own. If instead we let them know that we are available if they need us, then they can independently do their own work and develop self-discipline.

Being a resource means being willing to be interrupted when they need you. This approach is not necessarily stress-free. It's just a different kind of stress than the stress of policing children to do their work. The stress that comes from being a resource is that you may be interrupted any time. If you're reading, you may be just about to find out "who dunnit" when Charlie asks for help with math. How frustrating. But we have to put up with those interruptions if we want Charlie to view us as a resource. Listening to something our child has written, calling out spelling words, or asking the questions at the end of the chapter are all ways for us to serve as a resource.

Another part of the homework notices I have received from my children's schools stresses how important it is for parents to help their children with their homework. Some parents interpret this message to mean "Parents, when your children cannot do their work, do it for them." That's not what they mean. Grading children is hard enough for teachers without them having to grade parents as well. If you think an assignment or project is too difficult for your child, perhaps help your child break it down into smaller, more easily managed segments. Or discuss the problem with the teacher. Sometimes teachers do not realize their assignments are inappropriate until someone tells them. Solving the problem for children by doing their work only teaches children to rely on others and discourages self-discipline. There's a difference between being a resource for our children and doing the work for them. We can be a sounding board and guide for them, and we can channel them to the people or books they need for help.

REPORT CARDS

Report cards can also be the source of discipline problems. But they don't have to be, even if the grades are poor. Grades given on traditional report cards tell us precious little about what and how our children are learning. Grades, regardless of what they are, should be the starting point of a constructive discussion about learning, not the end product. These discussions are particularly helpful if grades are poor or have gone down. Let's look what happened between eight-year-old Eric and his dad:

ERIC: *Here's my report card, Dad.*
DAD: *Oh, my! I see you got four "Needs Improvement."*
ERIC: *I know, Dad.*
DAD: *Eric, you never got NIs before.*
ERIC: *It's the teacher's fault, Dad.*
DAD: *Never mind that, Eric. What are you going to do about it?*
ERIC: *I'm going to get all Es next time. You'll see, I'll get all Es.*
DAD: *I don't expect you to get all Es, but I don't want to see any more NIs. Do you hear me? I don't want any NIs.*

Is Eric really going to be able to keep his promise? Unlikely, unless he gets some guidance about his problem. How could he possibly be learning self-discipline? No one is teaching him what to do, how to correct his mistake. Let's look at what could have happened had father used the problem-solving approach:

ERIC: *Here's my report card, Dad.*
DAD: *Oh, my, I see you got four "Needs Improvement."*
ERIC: *I know, Dad.*
DAD: *It must be a disappointment, Eric.*
ERIC: *Yeah, it sure is. I feel terrible.*

DAD: *Why do you think you went down on those subjects?*

ERIC: *It's the teacher's fault, Dad.*

DAD: *What do you mean?*

ERIC: *She never explains anything, so I don't understand what's going on.*

DAD: *Well, Eric, if you don't understand what's going on, how could you help yourself figure it out?*

ERIC: *I could ask Sam. He seems to know what's going on.*

DAD: *Yes, or you could stay after school and get help from the teacher.*

ERIC: *Or, Dad, maybe I could go early to get help from her. Or maybe I could even show it to you and you could help me.*

Next, Dad could help Eric decide which of the options he would like to choose. The problem will be on the way to being solved. When Eric's work starts improving, they'll know that the solution is working.

In the second scenario Dad empathized with Eric, conveying that he understood how Eric must have felt, but at the same time he didn't let Eric get away with blaming it on the teacher. He placed the responsibility for learning right in the hands of Eric, where it belonged. Eric was learning self-discipline.

Punishing a child for getting poor grades only places pressure and tension on the child and on the parent-child relationship. Taking away allowance, telephone privileges, or socializing will not solve the problem. Chances are the pressure will do little to improve the grades, since the source of the problem is being ignored. Instead, if we as parents work together with our children to figure out what to do, not only will the problem be solved, but the parent-child relationship will be kept intact. On his own, the child may decide to limit telephone time so that he can get his work done. Such a decision coming from the child encourages self-discipline.

With respect to grades and report cards, we must also be wary not to demand perfection from our children. Sometimes when children think that they are expected to be perfect, it's difficult for them to complete any assignment. They keep erasing and changing answers because they never think that theirs is good enough. Teachers become frustrated with this behavior, and grades are lowered because of incomplete work. Some children feel that they will never be able to satisfy their parents' demands for perfection, so they just give up and don't try at all. "Why bother?" they think. Admitting our own imperfections and mistakes as well as not demanding perfection from our children are the most effective ways to avoid this problem. Remember, part of teaching children discipline means teaching them how to admit their mistakes and then how to replace their inappropriate behavior with appropriate behavior.

SASSINESS

Name Calling

What should we do when our child calls us "stupid," or even worse? (a) Punish him? (b) Call him stupid back? (c) Wash his mouth out with soap? (d) Just ignore him? or (e) None of the above? Yes, the answer is e, none of the above. We may be tempted to choose a, b, c, or d in the heat of the moment, but those choices will either not solve our problem or will create new problems in its place.

When a child calls you a name in the heat of passion, try to step back and not take it personally. Nasty names are usually a reflection of the intensity of a child's feelings at the moment and not his permanent feelings. Ignore the name temporarily (we'll get back to it later), but don't ignore the child and his feelings. Pay attention to what you think the child is feeling. "You don't like what I told you to do." "You're upset because we have to leave." "You are disappointed that you can't go out with your friends." These are responses that pick up and reflect back to the child his feelings. As we discussed in chapter 6, try to help the child get to the source of the anger and express it nonhurtfully in words.

Be sure that the child still follows through and does what you told him to do. "You may not want to wash your hands, but you will wash them before you come to the table." Don't let sassiness divert you from your initial request of the child.

After both you and your child have calmed down, then you can address the issue of inappropriate language from a problem-solving perspective. "I understand that you were angry, but calling me 'stupid' is inappropriate. The next time you are upset, what could you do to help yourself not use inappropriate language?" This places the solution to the problem in the hands of the child, thus teaching the child self-control and self-discipline.

Getting in the Last Word

Sometimes children insist on getting in the last word. If we play out this game with them, we'll never win. They can probably keep it up longer than we can. Anyway, why bother? Let them have the last word while we get the last say. They may give a wisecrack back just to top off the discussion, but as long as they do what we have asked them to, our ultimate goal is being met.

Arguing Back

Sometimes children deliberately get into a fight with us so that they have a legitimate excuse for getting out of doing something they don't want to do:

MOM: *Lee, supper's ready, come right now.*
LEE: *What's for supper, Mom?*
MOM: *We're having meat loaf, mashed potatoes, and green beans.*

LEE: *Yuk, Mom. You know I hate that stuff.*
MOM: *Just sit here and eat.*

The family is sitting at the table. Lee kicks his little brother.

MARK: *Ow! Mommy, Lee kicked me.*
MOM: *Did you kick him, Lee?*
LEE: *Yeah, so what?*
MOM: *So what?*
LEE: *Yes, I said so what. I don't care. He's a little brat.*
MOM: *Lee, stop talking that way.*
LEE: *I'll talk any way I want. Everyone in this family gets on my nerves. I can't stand it here.*
MOM: *Well, Lee, if you feel that way, leave the table right now.*
LEE: *Good, I'll do just that!*

What happened? Lee got exactly what he wanted handed to him on a silver platter. He couldn't stand supper, and he needed an excuse to get away from the table. Mom fed right into his strategy, and he was excused from staring at the meat loaf on his plate.

Sometimes children will be sassy back to us and keep arguing just to manipulate us into taking away some privilege they don't want in the first place. If instead Mom had acknowledged his dislike of the meat loaf and perhaps had suggested that he focus on the other items on the table, perhaps Lee would not have created such a scene.

A Word to the Wise

When it comes to children calling us names and being fresh, it's usually helpful to try to listen to ourselves. Do we call them names? Do we hear those same names being echoed back to us? Sometimes we may not even realize what we are doing until we see it reflected back in our children.

LYING

Many preschoolers often do not know the difference between reality and fantasy. What may seem to us to be a lie may just be normal thinking for children their age. A helpful response to their exaggerations and imagination is to point out kindly that their stories reflect their wishes and imagination rather than reality. "That's a good pretend story" or "Don't you wish you lived in a castle?" Calling their fantasies lies will squelch their imaginations and make them fearful.

Older children, however, can understand the difference between reality and fantasy. Their exaggerations and untruths are usually intentionally concocted to deceive. These untruths are the focus of our discussion on lying.

For older children, telling a lie often represents a solution to the child's problem. Understanding what kinds of problems motivate children to tell a lie is the first step in eliminating this distressing habit. Let's look at a few of the main reasons that children tell lies.

Sometimes children tell lies to protect their self-image. Children often feel that lies can help them mask their vulnerable points.

• Children may choose to tell a lie when they feel **ashamed.** Gretchen came home early from playing at her friend's house. She told her mom she didn't feel well, so she left early. The truth was that Gretchen and her friend had been bickering the whole day and her friend's mom decided to send Gretchen home early. Gretchen told a lie because she was too ashamed to admit to her mother what happened.

• Children may choose to tell a lie when they feel **afraid.** Someone stole Chip's money out of his locker. He told his parents that he lost it. He told a lie because he was afraid that if his parents called the school to complain about the stolen money, the one who stole it might find out and get back at him.

• Children may choose to tell a lie when they **feel insecure and fear rejection.** Kate never invited friends over to her house. She told them that she had a sick grandmother living with her and the noise would disturb her. Kate told this lie because she was embarrassed that her house was not as fancy as those of her friends.

• Children may choose to tell a lie to **cover a deficiency.** Michelle was very forgetful. She forgot to do her homework. She told her teacher that someone tore it up on the bus on the way to school. Michelle told a lie so that she would not be labeled "forgetful" or "spacey" again as she had been in the past.

• Sometimes children tell a lie **to protect themselves from punishment.** Kurt was playing ball in the house and accidentally broke a vase. He told his mom that the cat jumped on to the table and knocked the vase over. He told this lie because he was afraid his mother was going to spank him for breaking the vase.

• Sometimes children tell a lie if their **parents are too strict with them.** They feel they have to sneak to do what normal kids their age are allowed to do.

Sixteen-year-old Gil's parents would not allow him to go out with girls. On weekends he would tell his parents he was going to the mall with his male friends. As soon as Gil arrived at the mall, he left his pals and met his girlfriend. Gil told a lie because he felt his parents' rules were too strict and they wouldn't budge from them.

What We Can Do When Our Children Tell A Lie

♦ The best response to a lie is curiosity. "I wonder why you couldn't tell me what really happened." This approach makes it easier for children to tell the truth. Stay calm and encourage them to discuss why they felt they needed to tell a lie. "I lied because I was afraid that if I told you about the money, you'd call the school and I might get beat up."

♦ Separate your own issues and feelings from the discussion. Try not to overreact. When children tell a lie, many parents get very upset because they are afraid that their children do not trust them and that they'll never know what their children are thinking. If we overreact and get furious at them, then they will indeed learn not to trust us. Forget about the betrayal of your trust for the time being. Focus on the child's feelings that led him to lie rather than your own feelings his lie aroused.

♦ Don't blow one lie out of proportion. Refrain from labeling him a liar or overreacting and treating your child as if he'll end up in the penitentiary if he keeps up this lying.

♦ Listen empathetically to the reasons for not telling the truth. Rather than giving the message "You had no right to feel that way," try to reflect back what the child was feeling: "So you were frightened that something might happen to you," or "You were embarrassed." By listening empathetically and keeping our own emotions out, we may be able to gain insight into our children's fears and insecurities, such as with the child who tells the lie about having a sick grandmother.

♦ Ask yourself, "Is there anything that I am doing that causes my child to be afraid to tell the truth?" We want our children to trust us, but sometimes our overreactions to their behavior unknowingly cause mistrust.

♦ Try not to promise the child, "If you tell me the truth, I won't punish you." This is not always an honest, realistic promise. Instead, it might be more appropriate to say, "If you tell the truth, we can try to figure out what to do about this situation." The child will be more willing to tell the truth if he is not afraid of your wrath and revenge even if you do have to enforce a consequence.

♦ Let the child know that you know he or she is not telling the truth if you do know it. Say, "I understand that you did go to the store even though I told you not to," rather than ask, "Did you go to the store?" if you know full well that the child did. If your child is standing in front of a broken window with a baseball bat in his hand and a baseball on the other side of the window, what's the point in asking, "Who broke the window?" You know, your child knows, and a question like that will only put the child on the defensive and make it tempting for him not to admit it.

♦ Encourage children to be honest about their feelings. When children are pressured to cover up their true emotions, they will learn not to be honest about other things as well. We often squelch children's feelings from a very young age. Expressions like, "Don't cry," "Be brave even if it hurts," "Calm down, don't get too excited," "Say you're sorry even if you're not," and "Don't be so angry," teach children to be dishonest about their feelings. This dishonesty can lead to telling lies to cover up feelings. See chapter 5 for further discussion on how we can help our children express their feelings openly and honestly.

♦ Use the problem-solving approach to help the child tackle the problem that caused him to tell a lie in the first place. Ask the child, "How could you have told the truth about the money and still be protected from being beaten up?" Let the child work with you to come up with some alternative suggestions. In this case, probably the best solution would be for the child to explain his concerns to his parents and then for the parents to respect his fears and agree not to approach the school. Through problem solving, the child who broke the vase will be able to decide how to make restitution for it. Buying another vase will make him feel a lot better than harboring a lie in his conscience. As with other discipline issues, the key is to teach the child how to replace inappropriate behavior with appropriate behavior. Problem solving helps the child learn that he has many alternatives to telling a lie.

As with many other aspects of behavior, children do as we do, not as we say. It is unfair to have a double standard of honesty, one for us and one for our children. This means being honest with them as well as with other people in our own personal and business dealings.

If your child seems to be telling lies frequently, try to find a pattern to the lies. Do they revolve around homework? School? Friends? By detecting a pattern, you may be able to gain insight into the reasons for the lying. You can also try to make your child conscious of this pattern. Sometimes children will stop if it is brought to their attention. If the problem persists, then it would be advisable to seek professional help (see chapter 12).

WHINING

Whining can certainly grate on our nerves! Often children whine when they are not being listened to. It's a verbal expression of their frustration as well as a technique they think will grab our attention.

How should we respond to whining? "Ask me so I can really understand you," and "I can't understand you when you mumble that way," are responses that will usually put a stop to the whining. Also, some self-reflection may be in order. "Do I listen to this child?" "Do I answer her when she asks me something? Am I paying attention to what she says?"

NAGGING

Nagging is whining's first cousin. It's another tool children use when they think we are not listening to them. Just as with whining, asking ourselves if we are listening and paying attention to this child is an important step.

Children also nag if they think that persistence will drive us to give in and let them have their way. That's why it's important to be consistent in our discipline, think before we say no, but then once we say it, stick to it.

What about when we nag them? We're actually teaching them the benefits of nagging. When we find ourselves in the position of constantly nagging our children, it's just as distasteful to us as listening to their nagging.

How can we get out of the nagging business? First, get the child's full attention. Make sure that the child is listening. Word your request in a way that implies that you expect the child to do as asked. "I expect you to take out the trash" rather than "Will you take out the trash?" Then sit back and rely on the child to remember. If he doesn't do what he's supposed to, be sure to enforce the logical or natural consequence. After one or two times of experiencing the consequences, the child will most likely remember the next time. This is one of the ways that children learn self-discipline.

TATTLING

Yet another annoying habit of children is tattling. Tattling can not only annoy us parents, but also the siblings and friends of the tattler. "Mommy, Meredith hit me." "Daddy, he's playing with the stereo."

Not all tattling is bad. Sometimes tattling can protect another child's safety. We need to be informed when a child is acting inappropriately and may cause harm to himself or others. "Mom, the baby is going near the light socket."

Sometimes, children tell on someone else to determine if it's okay for them to be doing the same thing. Children may tattle as they are developing their conscience. This is particularly true of five-year-olds. "Zack's painting at the easel now" may be the child's way of asking, "Is it okay to paint at the easel now?"

Other times, negative motives lie beneath children's tattling. Some tell on others to show they're so good. "Scott's watching TV when he's not supposed to." Responding with, "That bothers you," helps us to get at the feelings that caused the tattling. By engaging in reflective listening, reflecting back to the child that he's bothered by the other child's behavior, we identify the true source of the feelings. This response might help you to figure out why that child feels the need to get Scott in trouble to make her look good. You might find that the child is diverting your attention away from something inappropriate she did. Perhaps she feels that the other child is favored or gets more attention.

Sometimes children tell on others just to get them in trouble. Rather than trying to make themselves look good, they're trying to make someone else look bad. Listening, observing, and thinking about the situation will help you get insight into the problem.

Some children tell on their siblings to test their parents. If the sibling gets away with that behavior, then they feel they can get away with it also. Here's where consistency is so very important.

As we saw in chapter 9, children are much more likely to tattle if we intervene in their fights when they come running to us to tell on a sibling. Keeping ourselves out of the battle by not taking sides and helping our children use problem solving to resolve their own disputes can eliminate this source of tattling.

TANTRUMS

Tantrums are a normal aspect of development—for young children, that is. They want something, and they want it right away. They cannot wait. Their verbal skills are limited. Sometimes the only way they know how to express themselves is to scream. The key with tantrums is not to overreact. Stay calm. Remove the child from the situation if possible. If not, don't worry about anyone else around you—if they've had kids, they've probably been through this also. Regardless, what's important at this time is your relationship with your child, not your relationship with the rest of the world. Then ignore the child's behavior but not the child's feelings. Try to put the child's feelings into words and figure out how to solve the problem. Sometimes you may not be able to solve the problem, but just acknowledging the feelings will help. "You're disappointed that we can't buy that toy." Giving in to the tantrum or getting overly excited when it happens will only make matters worse. The child will probably use tantrums to get what she wants or at least to get your attention.

Tantrums are most likely to occur when children are tired or overstimulated. While we may know that tantrums may result from exhaustion, it's helpful not to tell the child, "Oh, you're tired; that's why you're acting this way." Otherwise, the child may learn to use exhaustion as an excuse when he misbehaves. Many times tantrums can be prevented by monitoring a child's mood and not pushing him beyond his limits of patience and tolerance.

COMPUTERS, TELEVISION, MOVIES, AND VIDEO GAMES

"Why can't I? Everyone else does," is a familiar war cry when it comes to electronic media. The truth is, many children have unrestricted access to television, movies, computers, and video games. After all, electronic media are great baby-sitters. It can be tempting for parents to opt for convenience and avoid the hassle of saying "no." But the price we pay can be exorbitant. Children glued to the screen are not developing necessary social skills and in many cases are actually learning antisocial behaviors. Restricting television and movies to only those appropriate for a child's age and limiting the number of viewing hours per week (preferably to no more than an average of one hour a day) may be difficult but is really in the best interest of our children and of society in general. Banning violent video games and movies is the act of a responsible parent. Too many of our children nowadays view violence as entertainment. Unfortunately, we have all witnessed the horrific results of such exposure.

How can we monitor our children? We can't always, but we owe it to our children to try to do the best we can. One simple solution is to place televisions and computers in public spaces in our homes. Children do not need televisions, VCRs, and computers in their bedrooms. This makes it too tempting for children to hole themselves up and become reclusive. We also run the risk of having our children be exposed to psychologically harmful material without our knowledge.

For younger children, we can discuss our preferences with the parents of our children's friends. Assuming they think the same way we do is naive. When she was in third grade, one of my children attended a birthday party at a respected educator's house. I assumed that any video shown there would be appropriate. Boy, was I naive! My child had nightmares for several days after viewing that evening's murder feature.

The bottom line: While it may be tempting to entertain our children with unlimited access to electronic media, it's not in our children's bests interests and thus not in ours, either.

SUMMARY: FACING DISCIPLINE PROBLEMS

I am often asked, "How can I think of appropriate discipline measures on the spot?" By practicing the skills we have discussed throughout the book, you will be able to solve many problems spontaneously. But not always. Other situations may take more thought. All parents make mistakes at times. One important aspect of a successful approach to discipline is teaching our children how to admit their mistakes and change their behavior. We're entitled to do the same.

CHAPTER TWELVE

Where to Go for Help

PARENTING COURSES

Until we're actually parents, it's hard to imagine the challenges as well as the joys of parenting. Despite all the courses in child psychology I took while getting my doctorate, the most valuable training I received to be a parent were those parenting courses and lectures I attended as my children were growing up. Isn't it ironic that parenting is one of the most important and difficult jobs we will ever have, yet it is the job for which we receive the least training! All of us parents would benefit from on-the-job training.

NATIONAL ORGANIZATIONS

Many organizations provide parent training courses throughout the United States. Below is a list of some of the organizations that you can contact for further information on programs:

Active Parenting
810 Franklin Court, Suite B
Marietta, GA 30067

Phone: (800) 825-0060
Fax: (770) 429-0334
Website: www.activeparenting.com
E-mail: cservice@activeparenting.com

Active Parenting trains leaders of parent groups throughout the United States. You can contact them for information about Active Parenting classes in your area as well as about leadership training.

American Guidance Service
4201 Woodland Road
Circle Pines, MN 55014-1796
Phone: (800) 328-2560
Fax: (800) 471-8457
Website: www.agsnet.com
E-Mail: *agsmail.@ags.net*

AGS publishes parenting materials that include: Sytematic Training for Effective Parenting (STEP), STEP/TEEN, Early Childhood STEP, and Responsive Parenting. You can contact AGS for these materials or for information about where these courses are being taught. STEP and Early Childhood STEP are also available in Spanish.

Gordon Training International
531 Stevens Avenue West
Solana Beach, CA 92075
Phone: (800) 628-1197
Fax: (858) 481-8125
Website: www.gordontraining.com
E-mail: info@gordontraining.com

Gordon Training International provides parent training through a self-directed video program called "Family Effectiveness Training: Bringing P.E.T. into the Family."
Dr. Thomas Gordon teaches this course.

LOCAL ORGANIZATIONS

Many community agencies and groups conduct parenting courses. You can contact the following to inquire about what might be offered in your particular community: the school district central office, area hospitals—both medical and psychiatric—churches and synagogues, community centers, colleges and universities, technical institutes, the local or state child abuse council, and newspapers. Often, parenting programs are advertised on the radio and in newspapers. If you cannot find a program, you might try to encourage a school counselor or school psychologist from your child's school to teach one. Here are some factors to look at when deciding whether a parenting program will be appropriate for you:

- Is the instructor interesting and nonjudgmental? Try to avoid someone with a know-it-all, holier-than-thou attitude; no one knows it all. Remember, even good programs may hire poor instructors.

- Is it hands-on rather than all lecture? Do they provide ample opportunity to engage in role play and to practice new skills?

- Is it practical and realistic?

- Are children as well as parents treated with dignity and respect?

- Does the course focus on teaching children self-control rather than on controlling children?

- Is the course directed to the present age/s of your child/ren?

INDIVIDUAL OR FAMILY THERAPY

Sometimes a group course in parenting may not be sufficient to help us with some of the individual discipline challenges we face as we raise our children. Many other resources are available to provide parents and children with the help they need and deserve. If you find your child's behavior to be worrisome, if someone else such as the child's teacher recommends professional help, or if you are feeling extremely stressed by the challenge of parenting, then it might be wise to consult a professional who is trained to help children and their parents. Many of the most effective parents are those who are open and willing to seek the help of others when they are faced with child-rearing problems. We all need guidance and support at one time or another.

Children often express their feelings in actions rather than words. Our children's misbehavior, when it goes to the extreme or persists for a long time, may be their way of letting us know that they are in pain. Perhaps they have personal issues with which they are struggling. Perhaps the problem lies with the family dynamics. Perhaps the problem originates outside the home—in school or in the neighborhood. As parents, we are often too close to the situation to be able to figure out what's going on. Our usual approach to discipline may not apply. That's where trained professionals are a valuable resource.

We have many different choices when it comes to seeking help. School counselors, psychologists, psychiatrists, clinical social workers, marriage and family therapists, psychiatric nurses, certified mental health workers, and pastoral counselors (clergy) are all qualified to provide therapy.

How to Find a Counselor or Therapist

If possible, get a personal referral. If you know someone who has been helped by a counselor or therapist and you feel comfortable asking them, do so. If you don't know someone who is seeing a counselor or therapist, try to ask another person you trust for some suggestions. Good possibilities might include a school counselor, a school psychologist, a teacher, your doctor, or your clergy person.

If you can't get a personal referral, check out the resources in your community yourself. Check the phone book or call Information to find out the names and numbers of the local mental health clinic, pastoral counseling center, family service agency, hospital, or a university or college counseling psychology department. These places go by different titles in different towns, but the operator should be able to help you figure out the correct title.

You can call any of these places and ask for a referral. Many of them help people on a sliding-scale basis. You can also contact the following national organizations. They will give you names of counselors or therapists who belong to their organizations and who live in your area.

National Organizations

American Association for Marriage and Family Therapy
1133 Fifteenth Street NW, Suite 300
Washington, DC 20005-2710
Phone: (202) 452-0109
Fax: (202) 223-2329
Website: www.aamft.org
E-mail: central@aamft.org

You can find a therapist by your zip code at their Website.
You can also contact them to locate a particular state's AAMFT office. Many AAMFT clinical members will be listed as such in your local Yellow Pages.

National Board for Certified Counselors, Inc.
3 Terrace Way, Suite D
Greensboro, NC 27403
Phone: (336) 547-0607
Fax: (336) 547-0017
Website: www.nbcc.org
E-mail: nbcc@nbcc.org

They can give you a list of nationally certified counselors in your state. Nationally certified counselors have advanced degrees with specific course work in the field of counseling.

The American Psychiatric Association
1400 K Street NW
Washington, DC 20005
Phone: (202) 682-6000
Fax: (202) 682-6850
Website: www.psych.org
E-mail: apa@psych.org

You can ask for the phone number of the district branch in your state. The district branch will give you the names and phone numbers of some psychiatrists in your area. Psychiatrists are medical doctors who are trained to help people deal with emotional problems.

The American Psychological Association
750 First Street NE
Washington, DC 20002-4242
Phone: (202) 336-5700
Website: www.apa.org
E-mail: public.affairs@apa.org

Ask to be connected to the Public Affairs office. They will give you the phone number of your local state psychological association.

When you call that number, someone there will give you further guidance in finding a psychologist. Psychologists usually have received a doctoral degree from a university.

National Association of School Psychologists
4340 East West Highway, Suite 402
Bethesda, MD 20814
Phone: (301) 657-0270
Fax: (301) 657-0275
Website: www.naspweb.org

School psychologists are licensed or certified professionals who hold advanced degrees. They are trained to work with children, their teachers, and families. Contact them for information about school psychological services and a psychologist in your area.

The National Association of Social Workers
750 First Street NE, Suite 700
Washington, DC 20002-4241
Phone: (202) 408-8600
Fax: (202) 336-8310
Website: www.socialworkers.org
E-mail: info@naswdc.org

Contact the Clinical Register Office. They will give you a list of registered clinical social workers in your area. Clinical social workers have received advanced education and training to help people deal with emotional problems.

Look in the Yellow Pages under "therapists," "social workers," "counselors," "marriage and family therapists," "psychologists," "psychiatrists," or "psychotherapy." Getting a name out of a phone book is a bit risky. Just because someone has a title does not guarantee that he or she is the right person for you to talk to. At the very least you should try to find someone who specializes in working with children and parents. Today we are truly fortunate that so many qualified people can be found who are both able and willing to help us succeed in the challenge of teaching our children discipline.

Index

About the Author

Marilyn E. Gootman is founder of Gootman Education Associates, an educational consulting company that provides workshops and seminars for parents and educators focusing on successful strategies for raising and teaching children.

Dr. Gootman has appeared on CNN, MSNBC, CBS, Public Radio and on local radio and television shows throughout the United States and Canada. Publications as diverse as *Parents' Magazine*, *Newsweek*, *The New York Times*, *Moneysworth*, and *Reader's Digest* have solicited her professional opinion.

In addition to *The Loving Parents' Guide to Discipline*, Dr. Gootman is also the author of *The Caring Teacher's Guide to Discipline*, and *When a Friend Dies, A Book for Teens About Grieving and Healing*.

Dr. Gootman can be contacted at e-mail: gootman@earthlink.net